Black Cadet in a White Bastion

Charles Young at West Point

BRIAN G. SHELLUM

Foreword by

VINCENT K. BROOKS

University of Nebraska Press   *Lincoln and London*

Library of Congress Cataloging-
in-Publication Data
Shellum, Brian.
Black cadet in a white bastion :
Charles Young at West Point /
Brian G. Shellum ; foreword by
Vincent K. Brooks.
p. cm.
Includes bibliographical references
and index.
ISBN-13: 978-0-8032-9315-1 (pbk. : alk. paper)
ISBN-10: 0-8032-9315-1 (pbk. : alk. paper)
1. Young, Charles, 1864–1922. 2. African
Americans—Biography. 3. African American
military cadets—Biography. 4. Military ca-
dets—United States—Biography. 5. United
States Military Academy—Biography.
6. United States Military Academy—
History—19th century. 7. United States.
Army—African American troops—His-
tory—19th century. 8. African
American soldiers—Biography.
I. Title.
E185.97.Y63S53 2006
355'.0092–dc22
2005023689

For Paula, Kara, and Greg

Contents

Illustrations

Foreword

The annals of American history are filled with the names of our nation's greatest heroes, yet the name Charles Young is known by remarkably few Americans. Brian Shellum knows the name, and he reveals it—and the stories associated with it—to us all. In doing so he presents the fullest available view of Young to any reader who is interested in learning more about a truly great American. Born a slave, liberated by war, dedicated to pursuing excellence in a world hostile to his intent, yet undeterred in achieving the objects of his intent, Young serves as an example of extraordinary courage and commitment for all to behold.

Graduating from West Point against the odds and commissioned as an officer in the U.S. Army, Young became the third African American graduate of the academy and began a journey as the first to attain a full career of military service. Indeed, the significance of his graduation is even greater when one considers that no other African American graduated for nearly half a century afterward. Trailblazer, exemplar, mentor, professional, teacher, soldier, and statesman—all these words describe Young in his career of service to the United States. He carried the torch of equality and claimed nothing but the opportunity to serve his country honorably and equally. The torch has been passed from generation to generation, from leader to leader.

Young inspired the officer who became the first African American general and who was also the father of West Point's fourth African American graduate. He inspired his Buffalo Soldiers to precision, excellence, and greatness. He inspired people in the struggling country of Liberia where he represented the United States abroad. He inspired many American patriots by riding horseback from Wilberforce, Ohio, to Washington DC to demonstrate his fitness for high command on the eve of world war.

And Young inspired and continues to inspire countless leaders of our nation since his own day. I consider myself fortunate to have followed in the trail he blazed. My own experiences at West Point and my career of service to the nation since then are reflections of Charles Young, a true American hero whose story will now be told.

Vincent K. Brooks
Brigadier General,
United States Army

Preface

This book is about a forgotten hero. Charles Young was a mentor, leader, and trailblazer for African Americans in the military a century ago. Jim Crow and neglect are to blame for his anonymity today. I first read about Young's exploits as a military attaché in my initial year serving as a historian at the Defense Intelligence Agency (DIA). The DIA is responsible for compiling the history of military attachés, and I was keenly interested in the topic, as I had served as an attaché before retiring from active duty in the U.S. Army. Young and I also shared the same alma mater and branch colors. I attended West Point nearly a century after Young and donned the same cavalry yellow upon graduation.

I was immediately taken with Young and eager to learn more after reading the few short articles in the office files concerning his attaché tours in Haiti and Liberia. To my surprise, however, very little information was available, and what I found often contained errors and contradictions. Aside from a few magazine articles, web pages, and a self-published master's thesis, I could not locate a single serious study on the life of this important African American military figure.

I began learning more details of Young's life while assembling a large display on the Buffalo Soldiers in 1998. He had served with both the Ninth and Tenth U.S. Cavalry Regiments in the last decade of the nineteenth century and the first two decades of the twentieth. Young's service spanned a time when the Old Army was fighting the last battles of the Indian Wars on the frontier and transforming into a modern force to fight conventional and guerrilla wars overseas. In the following years I methodically researched periods of his life and presented papers at military history conferences. Somewhere along the way I decided to write a book about him.

I had originally intended to write a biography encompassing Young's entire military career, but after finding so much intriguing and unpublished material on his early life in Kentucky and Ohio and his cadet years at West Point, I decided that was the proper place to start. It was also a timely subject, with West Point celebrating its bicentennial. This book is the first serious effort to garner details of Young's conduct and experiences at the academy. In the future I hope to write additional books on Young's later years. His role is important enough to warrant that effort.

Part of the problem I encountered in writing a book on Young was the scarcity of primary source documents. Young's papers and diaries, unlike those of other notable African American personalities, found no central repository. Very little exists, and the bits and pieces are literally spread from Ohio to New York. I was told that many of Young's papers were stored in a shed behind his house in Xenia, Ohio, awaiting disposition, when a tornado struck and scattered the contents. Later, his heirs sold most of what remained of his papers and household goods in a public auction.

Young's passage from slavery to the halls of West Point is phenomenal enough on its face. He was one of only thirteen African Americans to gain entrance to West Point in the nineteenth century, and one of only three to graduate. Moreover, he rose to this accomplishment after being born into slavery in Kentucky. Although this is an extraordinary achievement in itself, it makes for an even more compelling account when examined in detail.

Why is Young important? He was the third black graduate of West Point, the first black U.S. military attaché, and, until his death in 1922, the highest-ranking African American officer in the Regular Army. For most of the thirty years he served in the military he was essentially the lone standard-bearer. The tale of Young's West Point experiences makes for a great story of success, but it also offers a sobering reminder of the effects of racial intolerance in our recent history.

Unlike the two black academy graduates before him, Young went on to a long and distinguished carrier in the military and achieved the rank of colonel. Only serious medical problems discovered on the eve of the U.S. entry into World War I—and some say racial prejudice—prevented him from becoming the first African American general. After Young, racial intolerance closed the door to blacks at the Academy. Forty-seven years passed before another African American graduated from West Point.

What were Young's experiences at West Point? It is easy to follow his academic and disciplinary record at the academy, since these are available in the official records. It is much more difficult to uncover details of how he was treated, how he responded, and what his classmates thought of him. Young never wrote a detailed account of his years at West Point so far as we know, and we are left with only general comments from his letters. Likewise, few of his classmates described how they viewed Young.

The reader will discern certain themes throughout the book. Why did Young want to attend West Point, and once there, why did he put up with so many difficulties to graduate? He clearly faced enormous challenges at the academy, both in terms of the rigorous cadet discipline and academics and in terms of the discrimination and isolation he faced. But certain people and key events provided important support to help him run the academy gauntlet. As a result, Young graduated from West Point and went on to become a forerunner for his race in the U.S. Army. If he had failed at West Point, he could not have achieved the enormous impact for African Americans resulting from his more than three decades of distinguished military service.

I almost missed one important theme until one of my manuscript reviewers reminded me of "the difficulty of tracing the life of a man who was usually invisible to his classmates." The challenge Young's life presents to a historian is considerable, and especially the period of his cadet career. Little is recorded about the lives of many important African Americans from this era, but that does not free historians from the obligation of finding the facts and telling the story.

The first African American to graduate from West Point, Henry O. Flipper, class of 1877, wrote a fascinating autobiography of his cadet experiences in 1878. Flipper was dismissed from the army in 1882 after a controversial court-martial, but he went on to enjoy a long and distinguished career as a civil engineer. John H. Alexander, the second black graduate, died a few years after he graduated in 1887 and left no known records of his experiences. That left Young as the only one of the academy's three African American graduates in the nineteenth century to enjoy a lengthy and successful military career.

A number of biographies have been written on important and influential African Americans from the nineteenth and early twentieth centuries. Books have recently been published on John P. Parker, one of Young's early mentors, and on W. E. B. DuBois and Booker T. Washington, both contemporaries and friends of Young's. All were leading members of the "talented tenth," and lively exchanges of notes with Young are featured in the published letters of both DuBois and Washington.

More to the point, *America's First Black General: Benjamin O. Davis Sr., 1880–1970*, was published by Marvin Fletcher in 1989. Young mentored Davis when he was a noncommissioned officer in the Ninth Cavalry and helped to prepare him for the officer's exam. Davis passed the test, was commissioned an army officer, and became the first black Regular Army general in 1940. Davis's dream was to have his son follow in Young's footsteps and attend West Point, and this dream came true when Benjamin O. Davis Jr. graduated from West Point in 1936, the first African American to do so since Young. To complete the circle, the younger Davis published *Benjamin O. Davis Jr. American: An Autobiography*, in 1991.

Scholars of African American and military history have sadly neglected this important black military trailblazer. Very little is known to most about Young beyond the basic outline of his life and experiences. Yet if it were not for Young, we may not have had Gen. Colin Powell as the first African American chairman of the Joint Chiefs of Staff or Gen. Vincent Brooks as the first black first captain of the Corps of Cadets.

Young deserves to be better understood and to receive the credit he is due. His misfortune was achieving a measure of greatness during the era of Jim Crow. I hope to rescue Young in some measure from historical obscurity with this book.

Acknowledgments

I owe the lion's share of gratitude to my wife, Paula DeMuth, for giving me the time and encouragement to complete this book. She was the first person I turned to when I had the idea of writing a book on Charles Young, as well as my chief advocate and most critical reader along the way. I also owe a great deal of thanks to my daughter, Kara, and my son, Greg, for inspiring and encouraging me as only children can. They forfeited a quantity of time with their father due to my work on this book. The only benefits they received in return were ready-made research for a couple of school reports.

My co-workers in the Defense Intelligence Agency History Office in Washington DC, Deane Allen and Curtis Utz, taught me much of what I know about the practice of research and writing history. Mirlin Toomer, a former co-worker in this same office, offered enthusiastic support along the way.

Besides the National Archives, four organizations provided the majority of the research materials and guidance. Dr. Floyd Thomas and the Afro-American Museum and Cultural Center have been a rich source of original research materials and advice. Floyd was also one of my most diligent and thorough manuscript reviewers and offered me endless encouragement. Alison Gibson at the Union Township Public Library proved a never-ending source of information about Ripley and provided critical contacts. One of these contacts, David Gray, took time out from turkey hunting to show me around the wonderful town of Ripley and revealed the Young-Gray connection. Lynn David and the Mason County History Museum were valuable sources on Young's early and family life in Kentucky. Lynn also spent a good deal of time reviewing my early drafts. Suzanne Christoff and her staff at the West Point Library Special Collections were my single most important asset in terms of research materials. Suzanne, Alan Aimone, Sheila Biles, Susan Lintelmann, and Alicia Mauldin were of enormous help.

I was fortunate to have a group of conscientious readers who worked over my various drafts. I have already mentioned Paula DeMuth and Floyd Thomas, but my sister Rolynn Anderson probably spent more time and evaluated more drafts than anyone else. My good friend Steve Rawlings also reviewed drafts and offered indispensable suggestions on imaginative connections and themes. Also, Dr. Phil Tucker made valuable comments on my second draft and offered encouragement. Lastly, Sue and Bob Parker gave my manuscript a thorough review.

Two individuals did a great deal of research and writing on Charles Young that were of great benefit to me in my early research. Robert E. Greene wrote an excellent master's thesis on Young, and his research was exceptional. Greene later published his work himself, and it remains an essential resource on Young's life. Nancy Heinl wrote some excellent articles on Young in the 1970s and collected a number of outstanding documents, which her son Michael shared with me.

After completing the initial draft of my manuscript and while laboring through the process of publishing, David P. Kilroy published *For Race and Country: The Life and Career of Colonel Charles Young*. Kilroy provides an excellent if brief overview of Young's complex life. But his book led me to an excellent source of original material that I used in my more detailed study. Jill and Malina Coleman shared a treasure trove of original photos, letters, and papers from the Young family.

I would like to thank the following organizations for their support: the Ninth and Tenth (Horse) Cavalry Association, Washington DC Chapter; the Association of Graduates at West Point; the Western Reserve Historical Society of Ohio; the Ohio Historical Society; the Parker House in Ripley; the Cumberland County Historical Society; and the Ripley Museum. Other individuals who assisted and encouraged me along the way include Amy Allen, Kevin Allen, John Birznieks, D'Arcy Brissman, Don Burger, Andrew Boyd, Betty Campbell, Tom Carhart, James Carroll, Deb Cibelli, Edward Coffman, Mary Collins, Tony Coleson, John Cooper, Betty Coutant, Theodore Crackel, Heidi Dickens, Geoff Drucker, Grady Dunn, Cheryl Dawson, Lee Edwards, Ward Eldredge, John Gatewood, Mark Gillespie, Jim Genovese, Martin Gordon, Stephen

Grove, Michael Heinl, Jackie Hite, Chuck Hoing, Axel Krigsman, Kathy LaCanne, Dave McSween, Montgomery Meigs, Holly Meyer, Bill Montgomery, Neely Moody, Marylee Myer, Berny Nalty, Mary Osborne, George Palmer, Antony Powell, Tim Rainey, Dave Rawlings, Jim Rawlings, Scott Rawlings, Judith Robinson, Dennis Russell, Kris Samsel, Rich Schwarz, Linda Settles, Colin Shellum, Steve Shellum, Richard Shuster, Scott Stephenson, Elizabeth Sullivan, Ann Trenda, Lorraine Warren, Carl Westmoreland, Mark Willett, Melissa Willett, Patti Wilcox, Karen Winn, Paul Young, and my parents.

Black Cadet in a White Bastion

Prologue

From the Jungles of Liberia

A man's real life is that accorded to him in the thoughts
of other men by reason of respect or natural love.

JOSEPH CONRAD

In 1915, more than twenty-five years after graduating from West
Point, Maj. Charles Young, Ninth U.S. Cavalry, reflected on his
time there in a letter to a former classmate. The world was at war
when Young wrote from Monrovia, Liberia, where he was posted as
the military attaché. He drafted the note to Col. Delamere Skerrett,
a fellow member of the West Point class of 1889. The letter, excerpted
here and discussed in more detail in the epilogue, is heartfelt and
telling.

After describing to his friend how his mission in Liberia was
progressing, Young thanks Skerrett and another classmate, Walter
Bethel, for remembering him at a recent class dinner at the academy.
Both had sent Young a "Menu Card and the other literary dope
pertaining to the Reunion." Young also notes that he intends to
write to his former classmates James Schermerhorn and Alexander
Piper, the former for sending him a "very interesting brochure"
from the reunion, the latter for "the repeated letters with which he
plies me in vain."[1]

Young then acknowledges bluntly, "You know for me the Academy has, even to this day, heart-aches in spite of the many advantages I derived there. The sole bright things that come to my heart
are the friendship and sympathy from men like you, Bethel, Webster, McGlachlin, Harrison, Lamblin, Langhorne, Barnum, and
Bandholtz." Later in the letter he adds the name of William Haan

to this list of friends and also mentions the "disinterested help of Col. W. B. Gordon and General Goethals."

He closes the letter, "I can never forget them; and have tried to pass along to others the kindness of you all, both in America, the Philippines, the West Indies and Africa. So you see you can not always tell the wide reaching influence of a word of cheer to even a black man. God knows how many white ones I have helped because you all helped me. Simply trying to pay the interest on the debt of gratitude, I owe you, that's all."

These intriguing passages shed light on Young's deepest feelings about his years at West Point. Despite the advantages he accrued as a graduate, the experience was tremendously painful for him, leaving wounds that remained raw a quarter century later. Through all the residual pain of his years at the academy, the memory of the friendship and sympathy shown by a small band of cadets shone brightly for Young. He was forever touched by the kindness of a small circle of classmates, and he remembered the humanity and decency shown by several other cadets and professors.

Young remembered first and foremost Delamere Skerrett, Walter Bethel, James Schermerhorn, and Alexander Piper, all members of his West Point class of 1889, who were arguably his closest white friends. He mentions other members of that class: Frank Webster, Edward McGlachlin, Ralph Harrison, James Lamblin, George Langhorne, and William Haan. He also names two members of other classes: Malvern-Hill Barnum, class of 1886, and Harry Bandholtz, class of 1890. Finally, he notes William Gordon and George Goethals, both assistant professors at West Point during his cadet years.

Although the journey that brought Charles Young to the jungles of Liberia involved a long and solitary struggle, his West Point experiences remained vivid in his memory. Unlike the rest of his classmates from throughout the United States, Young was black, the lone African American entering West Point, that white bastion of the military establishment. How did Young, who was born a slave, overcome the enormous challenges he faced in the years ahead? To answer this question, we must travel back in time to eighteenth-century Kentucky, Ohio, and finally West Point.

1. Enslaved in Kentucky

Tremble not before the free man, but before
the slave who has chains to break.

MARGARET FULLER, 1844

C harles Young was born in 1864 in the slave quarters of a small
farm in the Commonwealth of Kentucky. His parents were
still living in bondage when Charles was born, which made him a
slave as well. But while Charles's parents were born and raised in
slavery, Charles would grow up a free man. Still, it would take a
war and the sacrifice of countless Americans, both black and white,
to set him free.

Charles escaped slavery in Kentucky with his parents when he
was but an infant. Though spared the experience of the institution
of slavery as a child, he lived with its bitter legacy through his
parents and through the shared memory of the African American
community. To understand Young, it is essential to appreciate his
parents' experiences as enslaved African Americans in Kentucky and
as Civil War soldiers and refugees.

Gabriel and Arminta

Charles Young was born on March 12, 1864, to Gabriel Young and
Arminta Bruen[1] in Helena, Kentucky. On this day, Ulysses S. Grant
assumed command of the Army of the Potomac in a civil war that
was approaching its bloody end. Gabriel and his family lived in an
old log house on Helena Station Road long used as slave quarters.
The house lay near the small town of May's Lick in southern Mason
County, Kentucky.[2]

A settler named Matthew Gray had built this log house in 1792 as his original homestead when his family cleared and settled the land. He later built a larger, more comfortable house and moved out of the two-story log structure. At some point the house was moved or the land around it sold to a neighboring farm. This may have occurred when Gray died in 1836, leaving two farms in Mason County to two sons and a property in Ohio to a third. Still later, the structure was used to house slaves. When Charles Young was born the cabin belonged to the farmstead of James Willett, a member of one of several branches of the Willett family in the area.[3]

May's Lick lay to the south of the county seat of Maysville, which was situated on the Ohio River in the outer Bluegrass region of north-central Kentucky. This area, on the extreme northern rim of the Bluegrass, was a thriving agricultural region where hemp and tobacco were the primary crops. Slaves were central to the agricultural society of this part of Kentucky, especially on the larger hemp and tobacco plantations and farms.[4]

In contrast to slavery in the Deep South, with its sprawling plantations and longer growing seasons, slavery in the border state of Kentucky reflected greater diversity. Blacks constituted 20 percent of Kentucky's population in 1860, but many were employed in manufacturing and in the cities. Most farms and small plantations in the Bluegrass had at most only a handful of slaves, and only about 12 percent of Kentucky's slave owners kept twenty or more slaves. Prior to the Civil War, about 5 percent of Kentucky's African American population of approximately two hundred thousand were free blacks.[5]

In spite of these differences between Kentucky and the Deep South, Gabriel and Arminta faced no kinder brand of servitude. Although their everyday lives might have been easier than those of the slaves on the sugar plantations of Louisiana or the cotton plantations of Mississippi, this did not change the fact that they lived and worked in bondage. They toiled under backbreaking work schedules, suffered forced separation from family, and faced physical and psychological abuse. African Americans living in slavery were deprived of their civil liberties, with virtually every aspect of their lives controlled by their owners. In many ways, slavery for the

Youngs must have been even more onerous because of the nearness of emancipation in the free state of Ohio.[6]

According to Mason County records for 1860, one of the Willett families living on Helena Road owned five slaves and the other eleven. It is unclear which farm Gabriel and Arminta lived on or whether they were owned or "rented out" by the Willetts. It is also possible that one or both were owned by one of the Gray families who owned neighboring farms, since there was an important connection between the Youngs and the Grays after the war. It was not uncommon in the antebellum period for farmers, manufacturers, or businessmen to hire slaves owned by others for specific jobs or periods of time.[7]

According to later census records, Gabriel was born around 1838 and Arminta around 1842. Beyond this information, tracking the lives of Charles Young's parents as slaves before the Civil War is difficult. Records documenting the lives of enslaved African Americans are sparse and unreliable, and they rarely give full names. But sufficient records exist to provide at least an outline of the lives of Arminta and Gabriel.

According to one family account, Gabriel belonged to the owner of an adjoining farm, and Arminta lived on the Willett farm with her mother, Julia Bruen, whose maiden name was Coleman. According to this story, Julia had been purchased from a kindly French family named Byars, who provided her with some education. Julia had been freed by the Willetts, but she chose to stay on the place with her two boys and four girls, who, according to state law, remained slaves until they reached the age of twenty-one. The Willetts had several girls themselves, and Mrs. Willett and Julia raised their girls together.[8]

Another description of the family history claims that Arminta's father, whose last name was Bruen, was a free black man, and that Arminta's mother, born a slave, was freed when her oldest daughter was ten. The story continues: "According to Kentucky law, freed people were compelled to leave the State and the father went, but [Young's] grandmother Bruen refused to abandon her children, of whom there were several." Arminta's father moved to Michigan, where he lived for a time, but he later returned when "his thoughts turned toward his wife and children in Kentucky and, hanging his hoe on the fence, he went out of the gate and directed his footsteps whither his thoughts already had gone before."[9]

Arminta probably lived in the Willett home, with Gabriel working at a neighboring farm, and both helped work the places with a handful of other slaves. Gabriel was very good with horses, so he may have worked with the draft animals on the farm. On some of the smaller farms in this part of Kentucky, slaves worked alongside their masters of the middle class doing the same work. Even in that environment, the enslaved African Americans were subject to the whim and whip of their masters.

Work patterns varied in Kentucky depending on the size of the holding and the crops raised. Small slaveholders could not afford to divide their few working hands by gender and often sent both men and women to the fields. Hemp growers in Kentucky regarded women as physically unfit for the demanding work. With other crops, some tasks were reserved for women and others for men. Since it is unclear what was grown on the Willett farms, no firm conclusions can be drawn on Gabriel and Arminta's living or work conditions.[10]

Years later, the Willetts who were children at the time remembered Julia fondly as Aunt Julie and Arminta as Aunt Mintie. The term "Aunt" or "Auntie" conferred a special status in the household, indicating she might have been the head housekeeper, head cook, or nursemaid. The slave owner taught his children this designation of respect for trusted slaves who served the household and were in close contact with the children. There were clear delineations in the slave hierarchy, and field and household workers formed two separate groups. Since Arminta could read and write, it is possible that she was assigned as a personal slave to the children and learned by listening when they had their school lessons.[11]

In spite of this status, Arminta's life was fraught with risk and oppression. Enslaved African American women lived between the two worlds of the plantation household and the slave community, representing the cultures of the African American present and their African past. From birth, writes Elizabeth Fox-Genovese, "the slave girl's dual membership in the plantation household and the slave community shaped her identity." In a culture fashioned by enslaved men and women from diverse African regions and dominated by the master and mistress of the household, Arminta could never entirely shape her own life.[12]

In 1863, a former enslaved African American named Francis Frederic wrote a memoir about his life on a small plantation near Maysville. It is a sad tale of bondage and brutality, the sole bright spot being the ability of enslaved African Americans to maintain a culture and find hope where little existed. Frederic's experiences demonstrate that slavery could be every bit as appalling in Kentucky as elsewhere in the South.[13]

Frederic notes in his memoir the importance of folklore, music, and singing to the enslaved African American community. W. E. B. DuBois once said that spirituals "are the music of an unhappy people, of the children of disappointment; they tell of death and suffering and unvoiced longing toward a truer world, of misty wanderings and hidden ways." Both Harriet Tubman and Frederick Douglass maintained that many slave songs and spirituals carried double meanings. Others note that slaves in their folktales used sharp irony and strong symbolism. Arminta and Gabriel passed on this rich prism of folklore and music to Charles for use in his own struggle to find a truer world.[14]

Frederic's memoir provides a window on an existence that Gabriel and Arminta might have experienced. They were rough contemporaries in time and location and could have known each other by name. Gabriel and Arminta might have faced a similar sort of slavery in Mason County. Frederic failed in his first attempt to escape slavery and paid for it with 107 lashes. He succeeded on his second try, thanks to the intervention of local abolitionists who directed him to a way station on the Underground Railroad, and he lived out his years as a free man in Canada and Great Britain.[15]

Despite the U.S. Congress's prohibition on the importation of slaves into the United States in 1808 and Kentucky's ban on the importation of slaves for sale in 1833, slaves remained a lucrative commodity in the state. By the 1860s Kentucky was known as a "slave-growing" state, meaning it profited in the business of supplying enslaved African Americans to plantations in the Deep South.

The phrase "sold down the river" comes from this commerce in souls, since slaves were shipped down the Ohio River to the Mississippi.[16]

Frederic devotes a chapter in his book to the profitable slave trade in Kentucky. He passed from a kindly master to a cruel son after the former's death. The son went deeply into debt leading "a riotous, dissipated life, losing money by gambling, and then borrowing." According to Frederic, slaves were generally the first property parted with, bringing quick and hard cash. He gives pitiful accounts of children and infants being torn from their mothers' arms when slave traders came to collect their new "property."[17]

Fortunately, Gabriel Young remained in May's Lick and escaped the fate of so many other slaves in Kentucky. However, he changed hands locally, as is reflected in the will and deed books for Mason County. He first appears in an 1843 court inventory of property owned by the deceased Thomas Davis, which lists the following: "Black man Jerard, slave $250; woman Zilloe, slave $250; man Milton, slave $450; girl Martha $250; girl Emily $100; boy George $200; boy Gabriel $100." Gabriel was five years old at the time, and perhaps the "woman Zilloe" was his mother and some of the other children his siblings. There is no known record of who purchased or inherited Davis's slaves or whether Gabriel remained united with his family members.[18]

There is mention of a Gabriel joining the May's Lick Baptist Church in records that are undated but probably from the 1840s or 1850s. Among the "Names of Coloured Members who have connected themselves with the Church" are listed Gabriel and his owner, William Kemper. Gabriel must have remained a member of the church for a number of years, since many of the other names on the list are accompanied by remarks indicating they were deceased, dismissed, or excluded on various dates from as early as 1843 to as late as 1852. The white members of the May's Lick Baptist Church voted in 1855 to allow the 175 African American members to establish the Second Baptist Church, to which Gabriel presumably belonged.[19]

On June 7, 1864, less than a year before the end of the Civil War, Gabriel Young married Arminta Bruen. Rev. John Markam, pastor of the Second Baptist Church, performed the service and probably thought nothing of the fact that the couple already had a son. According to Young family history, the wedding took place on the large veranda of the Willett home and was followed that evening by a feast in the great dining hall. James Willett presented the license to the minister and said, "Now Mint you no longer belong to me, but to Gabe."[20]

It is clear that this marriage was not legally recognized in Kentucky at the time, since Gabriel was still a slave. Frederic mentions a few sham weddings in his memoir, but all were conducted informally among the slaves and none had legal standing. "Jumping the broom" was a common form of marriage in the slave community and was encouraged by many owners for the sake of harmony. Elisha Green, a Mason County African American Baptist minister who was also a slave, performed unofficial black marriages before the Civil War. Slave marriage was informal in the antebellum South, and only an owner's consent was necessary for slaves to marry or divorce. Some owners readily gave permission, while others did not.[21]

Civil War

Gabriel answered the call to arms and enlisted in the Union army in 1865, as did many other African Americans at the time. Perhaps he heard Frederick Douglass's appeal "Men of Color, to Arms," in which the former Maryland slave argued that "liberty won only by white men would lose half of its luster." Douglass also insisted that military service offered "a genuine opportunity to achieve first-class citizenship." In addition, the Union army offered freedom and may have been one of the few paying jobs readily available to Gabriel, who had a new family to support. He certainly had little or no future in Mason County, and the army offered him a ticket to a new life of freedom.

Kentucky was a border state during the Civil War. Although the state was pragmatically loyal to the Union, the vast majority of Kentuckians, many with roots or ancestors from Virginia or North Carolina, never favored an end to slavery and sympathized with the states' rights sentiments of the South. Because of its strategic position and the partisanship of many of its citizens, neither the

North nor the South respected Kentucky's armed neutrality. In the first year of the war it was invaded and occupied first by the Confederacy and then by Union forces. At the Battle of Perryville, Union forces defeated the Confederates in Kentucky and forced them to withdraw in late 1862, and thereafter Union troops occupied the state until the end of the war.[22]

Hard on the heels of Abraham Lincoln's Emancipation Proclamation of January 1, 1863, the War Department published an order that allowed the establishment of African American regiments led by white officers. On March 26, 1863, a year before Charles Young was born, Secretary of War Edwin M. Stanton issued an order directing Adj. Gen. Lorenzo Thomas to organize black regiments in the Mississippi Valley to support the war effort. Shortly thereafter, the War Department established a Bureau of Colored Troops to handle the recruitment, organization, and service of the newly organized regiments.[23]

This initiative came at a time when Washington was having difficulty finding enough soldiers in the war-weary North to fill the ranks of the Union army. During the Civil War more than 178,000 African Americans served in the Union army, of whom approximately 135,000 were recruited from the southern and border states. By April 1866, when the last of the blacks from Kentucky were demobilized, some 29,000 had been enlisted from the state.[24]

The enlistment of blacks into the Union army raised a firestorm of protest in Kentucky. Many Kentucky Unionists were slaveholders and felt the federal government had no business interfering with slavery in the state. Gabriel's owner was an officer serving in the Union army, yet he refused to give up his slaves. Kentucky at first even resisted the suggestion that free blacks in the state be enlisted, on the grounds that they were not citizens and therefore could not be used as soldiers. But by February 1864 the order went out to enroll all blacks of military age, including slaves. Resistance to the enlistment of African Americans into the Union army continued in Kentucky through the end of the war.[25]

Arming former slaves and putting them into blue uniforms was not a popular idea in Mason County. A *Maysville Bulletin* article in 1865 fumed: "Negro soldiers have never been of any service to the country and never will be. It was a disgrace to the nation that they were ever called into the service. The sooner they are all disbanded and set to honest labor the better it will be for them and the rest of the community. Laws should immediately be passed by the several States to compel the disbanded negro soldiers to go to work, or otherwise they will become the most accursed pest that ever annoyed society."[26]

The circumstances and timing of Gabriel's joining the army remain a bit murky. Charles Young clearly referred to his father joining as a "runaway slave." A family account written nearly a century after the event claimed he first ran away to a Union camp near Maysville to join the army, but his master rode into the camp demanding his release, "declaring him not to be of age and so he was returned home and hired out by his master." The price Gabriel paid for this act of rebellion is unknown, but perhaps this was how he came to be hired out to the farm adjoining the Willett place.[27]

Lincoln's Emancipation Proclamation freed the slaves in the Confederate States, but it did not apply to Kentucky or the other border states that remained loyal to the Union. The War Department initially exempted Kentucky from General Order 329, which provided for the enlistment of free blacks, slaves of disloyal owners, and slaves of consenting loyal owners in the border states. Because he remained enslaved in his home state, Gabriel fled north to Ohio, where it was easier to join one of the African American regiments.[28]

Before enlisting, Gabriel may have taken Arminta and Charles north with him to Ohio for their safety. Kentucky was generally a dangerous place for the families of runaway slaves, and it is hard to imagine Gabriel leaving them there. On the other hand, Arminta may have felt safe living in Kentucky with her mother, based on her status as a free woman and her close relationship with the Willett family. One family narrative had Gabriel taking Arminta first to Ohio and then back to Kentucky. An exact account will likely never be known.[29]

Gabriel was successful in his second attempt to escape, and on February 12, 1865, he appeared in Ripley, Ohio, to enlist in Company F, Fifth U.S. Colored Heavy Artillery. The clerk listed him in the

Company Descriptive Book as twenty-five years old; five feet, five inches tall; black; born in Mason County, Kentucky; and a farmer. Gabriel enlisted for a single one-year term and was credited to the Sixth District of Ohio. The Fifth Heavy Artillery was originally organized in Vicksburg, Mississippi, between August 1863 and January 1864 as the Ninth Louisiana Volunteers (African Descent). It was possible that Gabriel was part of a group of recruits sent to the Fifth Regiment to replace those whose original one-year term had expired or who were casualties of combat or disease.[30]

The well-known black abolitionist John P. Parker set up an office in Hillsboro, Ohio, to broker for black soldiers to fill the ranks of black regiments. Parker lived in Ripley and was thought to have arranged Gabriel's enlistment. Years later Young and Parker would become close friends, neighbors, and associates. On February 13, 1865, Gabriel mustered in Hillsboro with Capt. James Johnson's Company F, Fifth U.S. Colored Heavy Artillery Volunteers. Captain Johnson served with the Twentieth Ohio Volunteer Infantry before coming to the Fifth Regiment, as had many of the white officers and noncommissioned officers of the African American unit. Many white officers and noncommissioned officers readily sought positions in black volunteer units because of the opportunities for higher rank, responsibility, and pay. Gabriel's pay as a private was thirteen dollars a month.[31]

Gabriel's unit saw action in Mississippi, but for most of the year the regiment garrisoned Vicksburg, the site of Grant's great victory in 1863. The unit was "employed in re-burying the too-hastily interred dead and in cleaning up unsanitary places." An artillery regiment's assigned strength varied greatly during the war, but its authorized manning was 65 officers and 1,794 soldiers. In two years of service, Gabriel's regiment lost 4 officers and 124 enlisted men in battle and an additional 697 enlisted men to disease. But while Gabriel was with the unit, it probably experienced little fighting if any at all.[32]

Gabriel was one of about two hundred privates assigned to the company. "Heavy artillery" was a commonly used term for what was more accurately referred to as siege or garrison artillery, differing from the limber field or light artillery that accompanied the front-line fighting units. Later, some of these units were converted to infantry. As a private, Gabriel might have served as a cannoneer, who loaded and fired the guns, or as a wagoner, who moved ordnance and equipment with horses. He could have developed his skill with horses during his army service.

Still, no matter what their specific assignments, African American soldiers gained much more than practical skills in the Union army. They grew confident in their ability to carry out individual and team tasks assigned to them far beyond those inherent in the menial and unthinking life of slavery. Many also gained an education for the first time through the efforts of their well-meaning officers and African American chaplains. Lectures on everything from sanitary procedures to the Constitution widened the intellectual horizons of men long kept ignorant of such affairs.[33]

After twelve months of service, Gabriel was honorably discharged on February 12, 1866, near Vicksburg. Lt. Col. Lyman J. Hissong, then commanding the regiment, wrote this recommendation on the back of Gabriel's discharge certificate: "I take pleasure in recommending to the public at large the within named Gabriel Young. He has served faithfully and honestly, is a *Good* soldier, besides is trustworthy and reliable in every particular a gentleman, which is indispensable to a thorough soldier." This certificate was one of Gabriel's dearest treasures. Armed with this glowing appraisal of his service to his country, Gabriel should have returned to his family.[34]

Unlike the majority of his comrades, however, Gabriel did not leave Vicksburg when his unit mustered out. The muster record showed that he was paid through May 1866 and still serving at Vicksburg as an orderly at the regimental quartermaster depot. He must have made himself exceedingly useful, as he was selected to stay behind to assist in disposing of the regiment's assets. When he finally departed Vicksburg in May, he retained his army-issue knapsack, haversack, and canteen for the journey home. More importantly, he had accumulated about a hundred dollars in pay and an equal amount as a bounty payment—money that would enable him to buy land and start a new life in Ohio.[35]

Return Home

Gabriel had done well in the army, and the service had taught him a great deal about himself and other men. For the rest of his life he retained a fierce and unshakable loyalty to the army and country he served. The travel and wartime experiences broadened his outlook, and he acquired valuable skills and confidence. But with the war over he had to return to guide his family's future. The war was won, but the battle for black equality was just beginning. Gabriel's first challenge was to determine whether his family's future lay in Ohio or Kentucky. Perhaps the choice was not so difficult.

African Americans in uniform were not a welcome sight in Kentucky after the war. A postwar article in the *Maysville Bulletin* railed at plans to muster out black troops in Louisville and elsewhere in Kentucky. It detailed an order by Lt. Gen. Ulysses S. Grant to garrison southern seacoast forts with African American troops. The newspaper voiced the opinion that "it would have been much better if none had been retained in the service for any purpose, or if retained, that instead of garrisoning Southern Forts, they had been sent to garrison the military ports of New England, where their presence would have been less offensive to the taste and sentiments of the people, than it will be to the high spirited notions of the people of the South."[36]

The abolition of slavery in Kentucky after the war caused a revolution in social relations in the countryside, but "nowhere did a new order arise immediately from the ashes of the old." Rather, an agonizing period of transition set in, and in some tobacco-growing areas the old social forms persisted. Many whites in Kentucky refused to accept the new order long after the bitterest opponents in the Confederacy had been forced to yield. In fact, slavery did not legally end in Kentucky until December 18, 1865, more than eight months after Lee's surrender, and as late as the 1870s Kentuckians were still involved in litigation over the loss of their slaves. Kentucky was spared most of the physical destruction visited on many of the Confederate States, but changes in its antebellum agricultural society came slowly.[37]

African Americans in rural Kentucky faced a bleak situation in the postwar years. Aside from some marginal land and limited access to water resources, they were provided with few resources to meet the new challenges of living as free people. Most important were the formal rights of citizenship and the right to marry and have family relationships. But in many areas the former enslaved African Americans continued to work on the same lands and under conditions similar to those they had faced before the war. [38]

Clearly, Gabriel sensed few opportunities in Kentucky and decided his future lay to the north. He and Arminta could have returned to Kentucky and lived a life tainted by the past, as did so many thousands of other African Americans in the Bluegrass state. But he had seen the outside world during his year in the army, and he and Arminta decided to risk uncertainty for a better future elsewhere. It is easy to imagine Gabriel in his threadbare Union uniform, walking north with his wife and infant child to start their new lives in Ohio. Charles was fourteen months old when Gabriel returned home. [39]

2. Freedom in Ohio

It was not the physical part of slavery that made it cruel
and degrading; it was taking away from a human being
the initiative, of thinking, of doing his own ways.

JOHN PARKER

After escaping slavery in Kentucky as an infant, Charles Young
grew up in Ohio in two African American communities populated mainly by former slaves from Kentucky. Young was fortunate
that his parents eventually settled in Ripley, Ohio. Ripley was a
one-of-a-kind community, and the Youngs could have found no
better place in Ohio to start a new life.

The combination of parents, location, and natural aptitude provided a backdrop that maximized Charles's talents. First, his parents
nurtured him and took risks that allowed him to develop his full
potential. Second, his community and mentors helped expand his
talents and prepare him for an extraordinary future. Finally, Young
reached adulthood before the onset of Jim Crow laws, at a time
and place that afforded a window of opportunity for a determined
and talented African American. He seized that opening and never
looked back.

North to Ohio

Sometime after his release from active duty, Gabriel settled in Huntington Township in Brown County, Ohio. Huntington lay directly
across the river from Maysville, perhaps twenty miles from May's
Lick as the crow flies, but it must have seemed a world apart to the
Young family with their newly won freedom. It was also just a few
miles upriver from the town of Ripley, where Gabriel had enlisted
and where Charles would spend his formative years.[1]

Young family histories claim that Gabriel and his father, Simeon, went into partnership on a farm near Aberdeen sometime in the 1860s. One version of the story has the father settling in Ohio before Gabriel, but all accounts agree that they owned or worked the farm together for a time. Another story has Gabriel working as a tenant farmer on the land for several years after the war before he and his father could afford its purchase.[2]

According to family lore, Gabriel and his father initially "engaged in the menial task of cleaning up the flood damage before they had a roof over their heads" in "Slickaway and the Settlements." This may refer to a time before Arminta and Charles joined them from Kentucky. Later, "the family lived on Porter's place in the dilapidated tenant cabin—where the vermin and the rain either ruined their few precious belongings or worried them to their wits end." Years later, Charles spoke of his humble beginnings in the "settlements, Porter's Place, and Slickaway."[3]

The first definitive snapshot of Gabriel after his discharge from the army was recorded in the census of 1870, which described him as a thirty-two-year-old black farmer living on a farmstead north of the river port of Aberdeen, probably raising corn and a few chickens. His farm was valued at five hundred dollars and his personal estate at one hundred. Young likely purchased the farm and stock with money he earned and saved in the army, though he and Arminta might have put aside some money as slaves by working odd jobs and selling items grown in their gardens.[4]

Gabriel lived in a diverse farming community; neighbors living near him were black and white, rich and poor. On one side lived John King, a sixty-year old white carpenter, residing with his wife and three older children on a farm similar to Young's in size and value. Other neighbors included a black farm laborer named Joseph Thomas and his family from Kentucky, a white common laborer named Greenleaf Reeves and his family (neither Thomas nor Reeves possessed valued land or property), and an elderly white farmer named James S. Gray from Kentucky who possessed land worth four thousand dollars.[5]

James "Stewarty" Gray was the grandson of Matthew Gray, the neighbor who built the log house where Charles was born in Mason County. It was perhaps no coincidence that Gabriel moved to a farm adjoining James Gray's in Ohio after leaving Kentucky. This evidence is more compelling considering Gray was a fiercely partisan Republican and opposed to slavery. Upon the death of Matthew Gray, two of his slave-holding sons inherited property in Mason County, and James's father, John Gray, inherited the property in Huntington Township. James Gray probably helped establish Gabriel in his new life of freedom in Ohio and may have sold him the land that became his homestead.[6]

Other than James Gray, most of Gabriel's close neighbors were ordinary farmers, laborers, and widowers with their families. All three African American families in the area listed Kentucky as their home state, and one of those, that of sixty-seven-year old Peter Young, might have been relatives. These Kentucky ties were certainly important and comforting to the Youngs in their new home.[7]

A closer look at Gabriel's household reveals a great deal. According to the 1870 census, Gabriel was an illiterate, black male citizen with the right to vote, whereas Arminta, age twenty-eight, black, and "keeping house," could read and write. Their seven-year-old son, Charles, stayed at home and did not yet attend school. He was not noted as illiterate, however, and based on what we know about his family history he was home-schooled by his mother. A thirteen-year-old boy named Mason Branch also lived with them and was noted as "at home, adopted." Mason was also from Kentucky, but he could not read or write.[8]

Arminta's literacy deserves discussion, since it was central to Charles's education and so unusual at the time. In most slave states it was illegal to teach enslaved African Americans to read and write. Certain states even prohibited the education of some black freedmen and freedwomen. The few slaves who learned to read and write either did so in secret or with the permission of their owners who granted them a measure of independence and freedom.[9]

Arminta's mother, Julia Bruen, was responsible for her daughter's education. Julia had home-schooled Arminta, just as Arminta later home-schooled Charles. Born in 1817, Julia was credited as being the first African American teacher in Kentucky after the Civil War and was a cousin of Bishop Allen, the founder of the African

Methodist Episcopal (AME) Church in the United States. According to family accounts, Arminta taught Charles how to read the Bible and a church hymnal and later to "write and cipher." Julia sent papers and worksheets from her school in Kentucky to assist Arminta's teaching efforts, and from time to time she came to Ohio to conduct sessions herself.[10]

Gabriel and Arminta had good reasons for choosing Brown County as their new home. The area was close to Helena, which allowed them to remain in contact with friends and family in Kentucky. Gabriel was also familiar with this part of Ohio, since he enlisted in the Union army there and because many of the officers and men he had served with came from the Buckeye state. He originally signed on with the army through the help of John Parker, and the connection between the two continued and strengthened after the war. Without the Gray and Parker links, the Young family might have settled elsewhere in Ohio.

This part of Brown County was unique in having a number of resident abolitionists and a vibrant community of free blacks. Before the war it had been an important terminus in the "Underground Railroad," a term coined by slave hunters in the nearby town of Ripley. For runaway slaves from Kentucky, the area was considered an entryway to John Parker's "Promised Land." To Gabriel and Arminta it was the gateway to freedom and opportunity, though a great deal of hard work lay ahead.[11]

Ripley

Sometime during the 1870s, Gabriel moved his family again. He remained in Brown County but relocated to the small town of Ripley, less than ten miles distant. It is unknown exactly when or why he moved, but according to family accounts Gabriel and his father sold the farm and the latter moved to Manchester, Ohio. Perhaps Gabriel and Arminta saw a chance for a better life among the twenty-five-hundred inhabitants of the thriving town of Ripley. Certainly Arminta must have appreciated the better educational opportunities in the township.[12]

One possible reason for the move to Ripley is recorded in the federal government's pension records. On May 10, 1880, Gabriel filed for a pension based on his Civil War service in the Union army. He listed himself as an invalid as the basis for the claim and was granted an unspecified sum of money. Perhaps his physical infirmity at the age of forty was the reason he gave up farming. The pension and proceeds from the sale of the farm probably enabled Gabriel and Arminta to buy or build a house in Ripley.[13]

Ripley was founded in 1804 by Col. James Poage, a Virginia surveyor who settled on a thousand acres of land claimed as compensation for his Revolutionary War service. Poage homesteaded the land with his wife, ten children, and twenty slaves, whom he set free once he reached Ohio. Poage was drawn to this bend of the Ohio River not only for the richness of the land and timber but also because he abhorred slavery. He moved to Ohio from nearby Mason County, Kentucky, because he had come into conflict with slaveholders there. Other abolitionists, such as Dr. Alexander Campbell, soon followed, and by the 1830s Ripley was condemned from across the river in Kentucky as an "abolitionist hellhole."[14]

Another reason for Ripley's appeal to African Americans like Gabriel Young was the nearby settlements of free blacks. In 1818, 950 freed slaves once owned by a British merchant named Samuel Gist settled on about two thousand acres north of Ripley. Gist was a friend and business partner of George Washington, and he stipulated in his will that his heirs free the slaves on his vast Virginia holdings when he died. After his death, Virginia refused to let the freed slaves live there, so the proceeds of the sale of Gist's plantations were used to resettle them in Brown County. For the slaves across the Ohio River in Kentucky, the Gist settlements and the surrounding communities of free blacks were a haven and refuge from slave hunters.[15]

One of the men most responsible for Ripley's abolitionist reputation was Rev. John Rankin, who had moved to Ripley from Carlisle, Kentucky, in 1822 and carried on the work begun by Poage. During his initial weeks in Ripley he stayed with Colonel Poage's son Robert. In 1825 he published *Letters on American Slavery*, which clearly articulated his antislavery views and became required reading for abolitionists across the country. In 1834 Rankin founded the Ohio Anti-Slavery Society as an abolitionist platform.[16]

Between 1825 and 1865, Rankin and his Brown County supporters sheltered and facilitated the escape of more than two thousand slaves from the South. According to one account, twelve escaped slaves once hid in the Rankin home at one time. Rankin was reputed to have been Ohio's first and most active conductor on the Underground Railroad. His first home was a brick structure with three front doors on Front Street, facing the Ohio River, but he later built a brick house high on a hill overlooking Ripley—a better location for the business of smuggling slaves. Runaway slaves on the Kentucky shore to the south could see the light that always burned in Rankin's window, and they knew his door would be open and sanctuary assured if they could reach this gateway.[17]

Rankin founded Ripley College in 1828, and by 1831 it had nearly a hundred students from Ohio, Kentucky, and several southern states. The student roster included the sons of all the well-known abolitionists of the area as well as a number of southern sympathizers. Many of the faculty members and a few students led a double life and worked on the Underground Railroad. In 1831 Ripley College accepted its first African American student, Benjamin Templeton. His attendance caused turmoil in Ripley and some controversy at the college, and he transferred to Hanover College in Indiana the following year.[18]

Another famous alumnus of Ripley College was Ulysses S. Grant, who attended in 1838 and 1839. Grant was born in 1822 a short distance downriver at Point Pleasant, Ohio, and a year later his family moved to the Brown County seat of Georgetown. Young Grant first attended a "classified" school in Georgetown and later a private school in Maysville, Kentucky, where he lived with an uncle. That put Grant in Mason County at about the time of Gabriel Young's birth. Officials notified Grant of his appointment to West Point while he was attending Ripley College. He took passage on a steamer from Ripley in May 1839 to travel to West Point. Charles Young followed his footsteps forty-five years later, nominated from the same Ohio district as Grant.[19]

Ripley also took pride in the citizenship of the famous black abolitionist and entrepreneur John P. Parker, the same man who recruited Gabriel into the Union army and perhaps attracted the

Youngs to Ripley. Born in Norfolk, Virginia, in 1828, to a white planter and a slave mother, Parker was sold into slavery at age eight. He worked as a household servant and apprenticed as a craftsman in Mobile, Alabama, and then purchased his freedom in 1845. He settled in Cincinnati, where he not only worked in the foundry trade but also began a career as a conductor on the Underground Railroad.[20]

Parker started out his career as a conductor almost against his will. In 1845 he agreed under duress to help rescue two runaway slave girls, and in the process he was forcibly introduced to Ripley and the Underground Railroad. This adventure prompted him to move to Ripley in 1850, and there he joined forces with Rankin as an active abolitionist and operative in the Underground Railroad.[21]

Parker owned and operated a foundry by day and helped smuggle slaves out of Kentucky at night. He made numerous forays into Kentucky, scouting both sides of the Ohio River, and credited himself with saving the lives of 440 slaves. His daring exploits were detailed in his fascinating autobiography, and he was always in far more danger than his white abolitionist colleagues due to the color of his skin. Slave catchers were eager to cash in on the thousand-dollar reward Kentucky planters placed on Parker's head, dead or alive.[22]

Cherry Street

The second clear and reliable picture of Gabriel Young and his family in Ohio was recorded in the census of 1880. Gabriel resided in Ripley and was listed as the head of household, black, married, and thirty-eight years old. His thirty-four-year-old wife, Arminta, lived with him, as did their sixteen-year-old son, Charles. The adopted son mentioned in the 1870 census in Huntington was not listed. The balance of the census data reveal an intriguing story of a family and neighborhood.[23]

The Youngs were one of roughly ten families living on Cherry Street in the mostly poor and predominantly black neighborhood of southeastern Ripley. This impoverished corner of Ripley was bounded by the Ohio River to the south and by Red Oak Creek on the east. One block north and parallel to Cherry ran Main Street, the chief thoroughfare and central business district of the town.

Main Street ended at the Ohio River, and near this juncture was a municipal wharf that was used to ship passengers and goods for transport. Main Street ran west from the river to the outskirts of town past the large houses of the wealthy citizens of Ripley. One of these, a lawyer who lived in one of the big houses on Main Street, paid Charles to move cattle from field to pasture behind the cemetery every morning.[24]

A closer look at the Youngs' neighbors on Cherry Street reveals an integrated neighborhood with a great deal of diversity. Of the ten families listed in the census, eight were black and two were white. On one side lived a white widower named George Ashton, his five children, and a housekeeper. On the other side lived a black laborer named Harry Jackson and his wife, infant son, and mother-in-law. Among Gabriel's neighbors were farmworkers, a hotel porter, draymen, washwomen, river workers, laborers, and fishermen. Many of the African Americans who lived in the neighborhood probably attended the AME church on Cherry Street.[25]

Gabriel, Charles, and two of their neighbors—one black and one white—were listed as draymen, an antiquated term for a wagon driver. A dray was a two- or four-wheeled wagon pulled by either a man or a horse. According to family accounts, Gabriel had a small barn and ran a livery and feed stable. He was especially adept at taking emaciated horses, restoring them to health, and trading them at a profit. Gabriel and Charles also did odd jobs around the town and probably worked as draymen for John Parker, who owned a profitable foundry and had other business interests in Ripley.[26]

Ripley boasted a pork-packing plant, brewery, tannery, tobacco warehouse, cooper, foundry, sawmill, grain mill, gasworks, and a number of small businesses. Items had to be delivered to firms and individuals; goods were loaded and unloaded at the wharf. Whatever the work, it must have been steady for Gabriel and his white neighbor George Ashton, since they were kept busy during the census year, while Gabriel's black neighbor Horace Brooks was unemployed for two months.[27]

The census indicates that Gabriel was illiterate, as were the majority of the adult inhabitants of Cherry Street. All of the school-age children attended school, whether black or white. Most of the older children—between the ages of sixteen and eighteen—were already working but were not listed as illiterate, so it is assumed that they had attended school. Almost all of the black adults were illiterate, however—a legacy of slavery—with the exception of Arminta Young and neighbors Harry Jackson and his wife, Elizabeth. In contrast, all the white adults on the block—widow Mary Kendle, widower George Ashton, and his housekeeper, Mary Shanks—could read and write.[28]

Thus the general picture of Young's Cherry Street neighborhood reveals both diversity and poverty. Only a block from the main commercial street of Ripley, it was a world away in terms of opportunity and wealth. The poor blacks and whites of Cherry Street worked the bottom-rung jobs that were low-paying but essential in any town: they washed the clothes, held the doors, hauled the heavy loads, and did the dirty work to support the town's middle and upper classes. For Gabriel and his family, life in Ripley was not idyllic, but it was certainly far better than what they had experienced as slaves in Kentucky less than two decades earlier, and easier than farm life in the settlements, Porter's Place, and Slickaway.

Education

It is possible Gabriel insisted that Charles study hard and seek an education to raise him out of poverty. Perhaps Charles's literate neighbor Harry Jackson shaped his thinking. But according to most sources, Charles was principally influenced on the importance of education by his mother and his maternal grandmother, who supplemented his small-town education with instruction and direction of their own.[29]

Charles proved an able student in elementary school and received an excellent basic education, both in Ripley's public schools and at home. He was clearly born with a great deal of potential. According to the 1870 census, he was not yet attending school in Huntington Township at age six. He began elementary school sometime after 1870 and perhaps not until the family moved to Ripley. Charles likely spent fewer than six years in elementary school, supplemented with tutoring by his mother and grandmother.

During his years in grammar school, Charles developed a passion for music and learned to play the piano and the violin. For the rest of his life, his love for music served as both a social bridge to others and a pleasant diversion from his forced isolation in later years. Again, his mother nurtured and guided his natural talents in music, with echoes and melodies from her past life as an enslaved African American in Kentucky. This music of an unhappy people, rich with double meaning, would always be important to Charles.

Young family traditions also accord Gabriel with some of the credit for starting Charles along the path to music. It seems that one day Gabriel was plowing Captain Rankin's garden on Beacon Light Hill, made famous during the time of the Underground Railroad, and on his way home he discovered Charles and some other boys "dancing and vying for the small change cast in the street by some amused hand-clapping spectator." Gabriel was not amused at seeing his son panhandling in the street and said: "Sonnie! Go right in this minute. I don't ever want to ever see you at this again!" As a result, "That night Gabriel Young's dissatisfaction crystallized into the determination to buy a melodeon, the popular instrument of the day, and have the boy taught to play. He employed a man named Bloome as his son's teacher." Gabriel paid for the lessons with earnings from compost hauling and garden plowing. Charles made such rapid progress as a music student that he was shortly playing for Sunday school at the AME church and for both Sunday school and church services at the Baptist church where they were members. [30]

Much of the firsthand information available on the Ripley school system and Young's education came from reports in the *Ripley Bee and Times*, the local newspaper. According to a December 1881 summary of the Ripley Union school report, the system had 16 teachers, 714 enrolled students, 176 students in the "Colored Schools," and 14 pupils in the graduating class. The main school was located on Second Street on the public square next to the town hall. The African American school occupied two buildings on Fourth Street. [31]

Ripley did not formally integrate its school system until 1891, and while Charles was there it operated as one system under a single white superintendent, J. C. Shumaker. Some functions were integrated, but most classes were separate. There were separate white and black school principals as well as separate primary, intermediate, and high schools. African Americans made up about 25 percent of the student population and had proportionate number of teachers, four out of sixteen. The African American school principal was also the black high school teacher, J. T. Whitson, one of Young's early mentors. The other three teachers in the African American school taught grammar, intermediate level, and primary school.[32]

Some of the classes and educational activities were integrated, which was exceedingly unusual for this time. There was only one teacher of German and French in the Ripley school system. Young was exposed to both languages before his arrival at West Point (he was conversant in German and excelled at French), so it is reasonable to assume he took language classes in high school at Ripley in an integrated classroom. Also, the high school graduation ceremonies in June 1881 were combined and integrated. Charles sat among the twenty-one graduates who sang songs, read essays, and presented orations.[33]

Our only known firsthand description of Charles in high school is from the diary of Cora Young (no relation to Charles), the eldest daughter of a prominent white family in Ripley. Cora was one year behind Charles in school, and her father, William, was a respected lawyer, Civil War veteran, mayor of Ripley for ten years, and long-time member of the school board. William and Gabriel probably attended meetings of the Grand Army of the Republic (GAR) together, since both were "veterans of the late unpleasantness" and were active in the organization. The GAR was a powerful political and social force in the postwar period, buttressed by the bonds forged in battle. Perhaps the two elder Youngs traveled together to attend the fourteenth annual encampment of the GAR in Dayton, Ohio, in 1880.[34]

Cora's diary entries for February 24 to 26, 1881, provide a fascinating glimpse of Charles's human side and his struggle for equality. Cora was a white, upper-class girl who sympathized with Charles's fight for equal treatment and respected his determination and pluck. Her account focuses on a high school program for the citizens of Ripley celebrating the birthday of Henry Wadsworth Longfellow, who was born on February 27, 1807. Longfellow was well known at this time because of the easy rhyme of his poems and the popular themes his works celebrated. He died scarcely a year after the Ripley program, on March 24, 1882.[35]

The program was scheduled for Friday evening, February 25, 1881. The previous day, the students of the high school rehearsed their program under the direction of Superintendent Shumaker. The centerpiece of the program was an essay read by Charles entitled "The Shadow on the Blind." According to Cora, "Thursday afternoon when we were rehearsing, after he had read his essay, Prof. Shumaker corrected some of the mistakes he had made, and as Charlie looked over his papers to correct it, his hands shook like an aspen. He has my sympathies ever since for I know from that, that it was very difficult to get up before the school especially as he is the only colored scholar in the white school."

Cora's description of Charles's struggle in school that year is poignant and revealing: "Charlie is colored. He graduates with the white class this year. Some of the white scholars in the class 'cut up High' about him being in the class, for this is the first time the white and colored children have been allowed to 'mix' at all. The colored school always had a class to themselves before. We have many good colored schools here, and Prof. Shumaker is Superintendent of them as well as the white. Charlie has a good deal of 'pluck' to graduate for his white classmates treat him scandalously mean, and everybody, that is every white person, is very much opposed to him. He has the backing of the school board though (Papa is a member), and he is determined to 'pull through.'"

Cora describes the Friday event at the town hall as follows: "The hall was 'jammed.' The High School and Graduating class occupied seats on the stage. I presided on the organ. The event of the evening was Charlie Young's essay. . . . [W]hen he arose to read his essay, there was a murmur all over the house, and some low-down wretched's in the back of the house hissed. Now, Charlie is no fool but rather the smartest in the class and will no doubt take the honors. When they hissed, Mr. Shumaker stamped his foot and said 'these pieces are from the public schools—let them be respected.' They were quiet after that and Charlie did his part as well if not better than the rest of the school. He did a hundred per-cent better than the boys in the school."

Cora concluded her entry for the evening's events with this comment concerning the nervousness Charles must have felt: "you could not have told that by his voice for he read nearly PERFECT. But [I] look[ed] at his paper and it was trembling so that it was difficult for him to see the writing." She concluded with the assessment that "He is very polite and gentlemanly" and joked, "He is no relation to Me(!)" She then detailed the various songs and essays in the program. Cora was a pianist like Charles, and she had a musical part in the program. Perhaps their shared love for music helped foster her sympathy and respect for Charles. There is no record of whether the audience was integrated like the students onstage, and if so, whether they sat together or separately. Certainly Gabriel and Arminta must have been there to take pride in Charles's performance and pluck.[36]

Although the Ripley school system was not formally integrated, certain activities were mixed. This was perhaps due in part to the residual influence of John Rankin and his early experiments with integrated schools. Ripley does not fit the mold of other Ohio school systems. The early Ripley schools and other abolitionist schools that were integrated probably set a tone not necessarily found elsewhere. The school's liberal-minded superintendent at the time, J. C. Shumaker, was respected for his progressiveness and tolerance. Whether out of open-mindedness or for practical reasons, he combined certain school activities, such as advanced-level language courses, school programs, and commencement exercises. This in part prepared Young for his future challenges at West Point.[37]

Mentors

In addition to the crucial encouragement of Arminta and Gabriel and the unique opportunities provided by the town of Ripley, mentors also played a critical role in Charles's growth. The progressive character of Superintendent Shumaker has been mentioned, but two others also offered essential mentoring: John Parker and J. T. Whitson. After Charles's parents, these two were perhaps the most influential in Young's future direction.

1. Log house on Helena Station Road near May's Lick, Kentucky, where Charles Young was born in 1864 (Author's photo)

2. Gabriel Young wearing his Civil War medal (Coleman Collection)

3. Arminta Young (Coleman Collection)

ma Mère!!

4. Tintype of Charles Young at age ten (Coleman Collection)

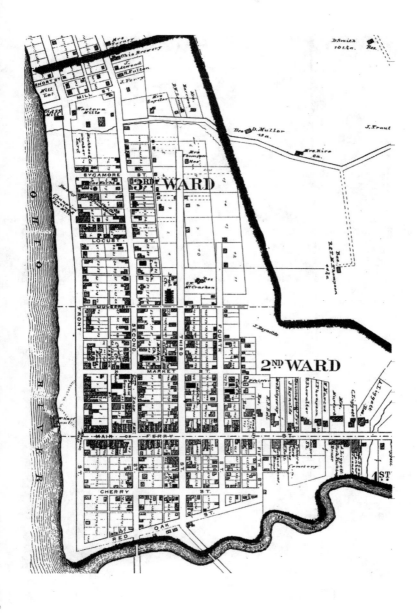

5. Ripley, Ohio, from the *Atlas of Brown County*, 1876
(Union Township Public Library)

6. Street scene from Ripley, Ohio, 1900 (Ohio Historical Society)

7. African Methodist Episcopal Church on Cherry Street in Ripley, Ohio (Ohio Historical Society)

8. John P. Parker House in Ripley, Ohio
(Ohio Historical Society)

Class of '81

KATE E. BELL.
EMMA B. HELBLING,
LIZZIE G. KINKEAD,
MARY H. MOCKBEE,
HATTIE DRISKELL,
LIZZIE LEGGETT,
ELMER GALBREATH,
G. G. BAMBACH,
J. ROBERT STIVERS,
CHAS. D. NORRIS,
ANNA M. BAMBACH.
SALLIE B. KINKEAD.
LOUISA J. SCHWALLIE,
BERTHA LADENBURGER
ANNA S. GADDIS.
JUDITH F. LEGGETT,
WILL. J. CAMPBELL,
CHAS. M. HAWKINS,
CHARLES YOUNG,
HERCULES MERRELL,
CHARLES LOWRY.

Board of Education.

PROGRAM

OPENING CHORUS, - - CLASS.

INVOCATION

SALUTATORY, JUDITH FIELD LEGGETT.

ESSAY—*My Boat is Launched, but where is the Shore?*
 —KATE BELL.

Instrumental Solo—"Venetian Regatta," (*Liszt*) Anna Bambach.

ORATION—*Self-Reliance*, - - CHAS. LOWRY.

ESSAY—*Simon says Thumbs Up*, BERTHA LADENBURGER.

ESSAY—*The Days of Auld Lang Syne*, LIZZIE KINKEAD.

ORATION—*Government*, - CHAS. NORRIS.

ESSAY—*Trifles not always Trivial*, ANNA GADDIS.

Vocal Trio—"Distant Chimes," } Lizzie Leggett,
 Mary Mockbee, Kate Bell

ESSAY—*A Basket of Chips*, LOUISA SCHWALLIE.

ORATION—*Ohio and Ohio Men*, ELMER GALBREATH.

ESSAY—*The Teachings of Nature*, HATTIE DRISKELL.

ESSAY—*Leaves have their time to fall*, SALLIE KINKEAD.

ORATION—*Pluck*, - CHAS. M. HAWKINS.

Instrumental Duet—"Militaire Galop," Lizzie and Sallie Kinkead.

ESSAY—*Deep Sea Soundings*, ANNA BAMBACH.

ORATION—*Let there be Light*, - CHAS. YOUNG.

ESSAY—*Golden Deeds*, - EMMA HELBLING.

ORATION—*American Inventions*, HERCULES MERRELL.

ESSAY—*Only a Girl—what can she do?* JUDITH LEGGETT.

ORATION—*The Achievements of Young Men*.
 GOTTLIEB BAMBACH.

Vocal Duet—"Two Alpine Maids," Lizzie and Judith Leggett.

ESSAY—*What Next?* - Mary H. Mockbee.

ORATION—*Surroundings*. Will. J. Campbell.

ESSAY—*Weep not that the World changes: did it keep a stable,
 changeless course, 'twere cause to weep*. Lizzie Leggett.

ORATION—*Education*, - Robert Stivers.

VALEDICTORY, KATE E. BELL.

Baccalaureate Address and Presentation of Diplomas,
 —Rev. J. M. Coskins.

CHORUS—"The Happy Wanderer," CLASS.

BENEDICTION

9. Ripley High School commencement program from June 2, 1881 (Union Township Public Library)

Strong evidence points to a close connection between Charles and John Parker. According to a March 29, 1876, article in the *Ripley Bee*, Charles was enrolled in the African American high school and led the school academically, while John Parker's daughter Hortense had the second-highest standing. Hortense was later one of the first African American graduates of Mount Holyoke College in South Hadley, Massachusetts.[38] Also, John Parker mentions in a letter that Charles used Parker's extensive private library in Ripley.[39] It would be surprising indeed if one of the most gifted African American students in Ripley was not mentored and encouraged by a man of Parker's strong beliefs. Parker's home faced the Ohio River on Front Street, and the walk for Charles from school or his house on Cherry Street was just a few blocks.

Young was a member of the Ripley High School class of 1881 when it celebrated its commencement at the Third Street Baptist Church on June 2, 1881. The invitation heralded the event as the "Tenth Annual Commencement of the Ripley High School." It is significant that the commencement program was integrated, with students celebrating together, sitting together on the stage, as they had earlier in the year for the Longfellow program. Charles shared the stage with twenty white classmates. One wonders if the parents sat together also.[40]

The graduation program itself was long and laden with activities. Each of the twenty-one students was expected to present an oration or essay, and some also sang or played instruments. Although no musical credits were listed in the program, Young probably played the piano to accompany his classmates' songs and duets, which included "Distant Chimes," "Two Alpine Maids," and "Militaire Galop." The program lasted three hours, but according to the *Bee*, "there was so much to commend and so little to criticize."[41]

Young's formal part was an oration entitled "Let There Be Light." Charles's white classmate Hercules Merrell talked about "American Inventions," surely spotlighting Ripley's own John Parker, who owned at least three of the seventy-seven patents issued to African Americans before 1886. Charles Hawkins gave a speech entitled "Pluck," something Cora Young thought Charles had in the right measure. And the valedictorian address by Kate Bell—"My Boat

Is Launched, But Where Is the Shore?"—could easily have been Young's theme for his future.[42]

After graduating from high school with honors, Young taught at the African American school in Ripley for several years. Beginning in the fall of 1881, he taught as the "Colored Intermediate" teacher, working under the guidance of J. T. Whitson, the de facto superintendent of the black schools in Ripley. As proof of the importance he attached to education, Young presented a paper entitled "We Must Educate" during one of the monthly teachers' meetings during the year. These meetings were also integrated, indicating that teachers in Ripley were far more progressive than society at large.[43]

According to Young family lore, "Part of the very first salary he [Charles] received was expended upon a plain gold ring for his mother." This was surely a token of gratitude for all of the sacrifices she had made for him. After moving to Ripley, Arminta had taken in sewing work to help with the family finances, and Charles had helped her with this work when he was a student. As a teacher he no longer had time to help her with the sewing, so he persuaded his mother to give up the work. To offset the loss of income, Charles ensured that "every month twelve of his munificent salary of thirty-five dollars found their way to the mother's purse."[44]

Charles taught again at the intermediate school in 1882. His grade book indicates instruction in reading, general history, geography, arithmetic, physical geography, grammar, spelling, American literature, descriptive geography, physiology, algebra, and U.S. history. Among his students was John Parker's youngest daughter, Bianca, who went on to study music after graduation.[45]

The year 1883 proved a formative one for Charles. He continued as an active and influential member of the teaching staff in the Ripley Union school system, and that summer the board selected him for another term as a teacher, this time in the "Colored Grammar" school. For this, Young passed an exam and was awarded a teaching certificate good for three years. He also stepped in that year as acting superintendent of the African American schools when J. T. Whitson resigned to devote himself to the study of medicine. Young could have stayed in Ripley and led a comfortable life as an educator and local leader of the black community, but he had already made a decision that would take him far from his bucolic life in Ohio.[46]

Sometime in early 1883, when Charles was pondering his future, he read an advertisement in the *Ripley Bee* concerning competitive examinations for West Point. Coincidentally, these exams were held in Hillsboro, Ohio, where his father had been mustered during the Civil War some eighteen years earlier. The decision to take this test could not have been an easy one for Charles, and he likely discussed the possibility with those most influential in his life.

One of Young's biographers asserts that it was Whitson who initially saw the advertisement and encouraged Charles to take advantage of the opportunity to obtain a free college education. This same source claims that Young's mother opposed the idea of a military life for her son. One can only imagine that Charles's father encouraged him both in terms of the educational opportunity and the military prospect, since Gabriel's service in the army had been a positive experience that provided him a new start in life.[47]

Young family tradition credits Gabriel with spotting the advertisement in the *Ripley Bee* and encouraging his son to take the test. According to this account, "Immediately a wave of ambition for his own son, confidence in the lad's ability, and hope for the large success for him surged through his father-heart. When the time for the examination came, the father hitched his fastest horses, not half so fleet however, as the flight of his fancy, and went with his son to Hillsboro, the testing place."[48] It is likely that Young also discussed the opportunity with John Parker and other people in Ripley. According to one of Young's military colleagues, Parker "helped Young to nurture his love for learning. . . . Mr. Parker was more than Young's scholastic mentor, he perhaps more than anyone else, helped Young to decide upon a military career."[49]

Beyond the encouragement of his father and mentors like Whitson and Parker, why would Charles want to attend West Point at all? He was an intellectual and valued education above all else. There were not many of the best institutions of higher learning open to a black man in 1883, and none save West Point were free. This was perhaps the key factor in Young's decision to seek an appointment there, but it was by no means the only one. In any case, Charles would soon discover that the education was not exactly free.

Charles must have seen his attendance at West Point and eventual commissioning as an officer in the Regular Army as a way to advance his race. His father was a living example of what the army could do to lift a black man out of slavery. Some of Gabriel's fellow black veterans had signed on as noncommissioned officers in positions of leadership in the four African American regiments after the Civil War. Other qualified African Americans were granted commissions in these units, mostly as chaplains. But at least one of these had graduated from West Point and been commissioned in the cavalry. So this was Charles Young's marker.

Nomination

Charles decided to take the academy examination and traveled the thirty-seven miles to Hillsboro in April 1883 in his father's wagon. According to the *Hillsboro Herald*, twenty-six young men took the physical exam and written test that lasted from 11 a.m. until late at night. Two African Americans were among the contenders: Young and Eugene Reynolds, who was from Adamson in Ross County. One of Young's white high school classmates, Charles Lowery, also took the exam.

Eleven out of the twenty-six scored a perfect one hundred on the written test, and it is likely that Young was one of them. William A. Stamats, who was white and listed as the "son of a soldier of Clinton County," scored highest overall and was the successful candidate. Young received the second-highest score and was designated the alternate, though the *Bee* did not mention that he was also the son of a soldier.[50]

U.S. Congressman Alphonso Hart from Ohio organized the physical exam and written test in Hillsboro to identify the best-qualified young man from the district to attend West Point. Each congressional district was entitled to have one cadet at the academy at any one time. The individual had to be a resident of the district, and appointments were made by the secretary of war at the request of the representative in Congress. Congressman Hart, the newly elected Republican representative of Ohio's Twelfth District, appointed Stamats to West Point. Stamats passed the academy entrance exam and was admitted with the class of 1887 on July 1, 1883.[51]

Considering the time, Congressman Hart might easily have picked Young instead of Stamats. The Republican Party in the postwar era was actively courting the black vote. It was the party of Abraham Lincoln, who had eliminated slavery and granted African Americans the right to vote, and black majorities helped elect Republicans in the South to Congress during Reconstruction (1867–77). Soon after the departure of the last federal troops, however, southern whites and Democrats reestablished hegemony in the South and began the systematic disfranchisement of African Americans. In Ohio, however, Republican congressmen like Hart still counted on the black vote in areas that had large African American populations.[52]

Proof of the Republican Party's connection with African Americans in Ripley was shown in the delegates to the Republican primary in 1881. The *Bee* listed John P. Parker and Gabriel Young among the delegates at the Republican primary for Union Township in 1881. The delegates elected Parker, Young, and thirty-one others to represent Ripley at the county convention in Georgetown on August 13, 1881. Neither made it to the state level as delegates, but they were among good company with old abolitionist names like Gilliland and Campbell.[53]

Even though African Americans in Ohio did not find themselves the victims of the same discrimination, proscription, and mob violence that would soon be commonplace in the South, prejudice was still present in the state. The atmosphere in Ripley was best illustrated by a story from the summer of 1883 involving an African American fugitive on the run from Kentucky. Under the headline "Arrested on an Ugly Charge," the *Bee* summarized the story of a black man named Samuel Bulger who was apprehended near the mouth of Red Oak Creek, not far from the Young house. Bulger was charged with assaulting a twelve-year-old white girl in a rural area not far from Charles's birthplace. He stole a boat, followed the old Underground Railroad route from Kentucky to Ohio, and probably stopped in Ripley to secure shelter from friends or relatives. The 1880 census showed at least one African American family with the name Bulger residing in Ripley.

After Bulger was captured the Ripley marshal conveyed him under armed escort to Maysville, but he transferred Bulger back to Ripley when a mob threatened him with lynching. Bulger then escaped, was recaptured, charged in local court, and transferred to another jurisdiction when another armed mob hijacked a steamer in Maysville and headed up the Ohio River for Ripley. The article assumed Bulger's guilt and never hinted that he was innocent until proven guilty, though the *Bee* clearly disdained the mob mentality of Maysville. How the Young household viewed these developments is unknown.[54]

Events at West Point soon caused Charles to move his thoughts beyond Ripley. For reasons not specified in the academy's records, William Stamats resigned from West Point on January 8, 1884. Congressman Hart had a vacancy to fill, and he notified Charles that he intended to nominate him based on his alternate status. The *Bee* reported that Stamats "failed in some way to pass muster, and Charlie, standing second on the list, has been given his place." Prior to being notified of the vacancy, Charles had gone home to Ripley and continued his teaching career. He must have been pleasantly surprised to learn that the son of a soldier from Brown County would get his chance after all.[55]

Congressman Hart nominated Young for the appointment on April 29, 1884, and Charles acknowledged receipt of the notification and accepted on May 10. On the same document, Gabriel assented to the acceptance of his son's appointment and gave permission for his son to "sign articles binding himself to serve the United States eight years, unless sooner discharged." The War Department officially appointed Young on May 28 and instructed him to report to West Point on June 10, 1884.[56]

Charles departed for West Point on Monday, June 2, and likely traveled to the East Coast by train. On June 4 the *Bee* featured a notice on the front page: "Chas. Young took his departure Monday evening for West Point. We wish Charley success in his new undertaking." Certainly his family, friends, and mentors gave him a suitable send-off. The teachers in Ripley would have held a departure event, and perhaps John Parker hosted a farewell party in his home on Front Street.[57]

Charles's parents probably took him to the Cincinnati train station in Gabriel's wagon, again hitched with the fastest horses. Or Charles may have taken a boat to Maysville and caught the Kentucky Central when it stopped on its way from Cincinnati to Richmond. From there he likely traveled by train to New York City, a journey of several days at least. From New York City he doubtless caught a locomotive north along the Hudson River to West Point.

To Charles's mother, now thirty-eight, bidding farewell to her only son must have been a tearful occasion. Ironically, Arminta was against his joining the military but largely responsible for the education that earned him his entrance to the academy. Gabriel, on the other hand, probably viewed more realistically the military aspect of his son's future. He had campaigned and traveled with the army, and perhaps he had encountered West Point–trained officers during the war. Still, neither would have been pleased to know that two years would pass before they would lay eyes on their son again.

As he took leave of his parents, Charles must have been full of excitement and trepidation. He had probably never ventured far from Kentucky and Ohio. Although New York was far from home, he had come even further since his humble birth as an enslaved African American in Kentucky. West Point instructed nominees to travel light and leave behind unnecessary baggage, as these would be of no use in their new lives, but Charles must have felt that he brought with him the hopes of his family and friends in Ripley as well as the dreams of African Americans throughout the country.

3. Beast Barracks and Plebe Year

> I have hardly ever known a mathematician
> who was capable of reasoning.
>
> PLATO

After making the long journey to New York City in June 1884, Charles continued by rail north along the east side of the Hudson River to the port of Garrison. This picturesque town in the Hudson Highlands was a short ferry trip across the river from West Point. It is easy to imagine his exhilaration and nervousness as he stepped off the train and got his first glimpse of the stark beauty of the academy across the river. Like a gothic fortress, West Point perched menacingly over a bend in the Hudson River. The post was established on this rocky promontory in 1778 not because of its splendor but for its natural advantage as a fortress on the waterway that cleaved the colonies during the American Revolution.[1]

Young could not have imagined the enormous challenges he would face in the year ahead in this hauntingly beautiful place. First he would have to endure the academic and medical examinations, which many of his prospective classmates would fail. He would then face two summer months of demanding military indoctrination and ritualized hazing, intended to transform civilians into cadets and eliminate those with too little resolve. If he survived the summer ordeal, he would confront an academic year meant to test his intellect to the fullest. All of these challenges would be made more difficult given the unfavorable treatment afforded African Americans at West Point. His character would be tested like never before.

Entrance Exam

Many of Young's future classmates arrived at the same time to take the entrance examinations scheduled from June 10 to 14, so Charles was probably not alone on the ferry. Nor was he the only African American among the nominees who took the long walk up the road from the ferry to the Plain of West Point: there were two others. But West Point did not expect all of the 130 young nominees from thirty-six states and territories in the Union scheduled to take the examination to pass.

A medical board composed of three U.S. Army medical officers assembled at West Point to screen the candidates' physical qualifications. The board admitted no cadet unless "he possessed the requisite physical ability to serve his country in the arduous and laborious station of a military officer, not only at the time of his admission, but during his life, until age shall disable him." Additionally, the academy required that the candidate be unmarried, between seventeen and twenty-two years of age, stand at least five feet tall, and be "free from any infectious or immoral disorder, and generally, from any deformity, disease, or infirmity, which may render them unfit for military service."[2]

No known official physical descriptions of Young as a cadet have survived. The three photos of him in this book show him to be a handsome African American man of medium height and slim build. One classmate described him as a "rather awkward, overgrown lad, large-boned and robust in physique," but that would fit most young men of that age. A copy of the only surviving official U.S. Army physical, taken when Young was fifty-three years old, listed him as five feet, eight inches tall and 154 pounds. So he was probably that height and perhaps a little leaner as a cadet.[3]

West Point scheduled the academic examination of candidates to follow immediately after the annual testing of the Corps of Cadets, the official name for the combined four classes of cadets, often referred to as "the corps." The regular staff and faculty of the academy, fresh from grilling the resident cadets, conducted the entrance assessment, a battery of written and oral tests in reading, writing, orthography (spelling), grammar, arithmetic, geography, and history. The oral tests required Young to stand in front of a panel of instructors and explain his answers or elucidate on a chalkboard. This must have been a nerve-racking experience for even the most educated and confident candidates.[4]

William Lassiter, who would become one of Young's classmates the following year, framed this initial picture of West Point: "My initiation to West Point was like being hurled suddenly from a group of loving and admiring relatives and friends into a den of lions. The cadets paid little attention to us new cadets until the result of the examinations was announced. At their conclusion, we stood in line, a miscellaneous, motley lot, dressed in all varieties of civilian garments. While we trembled in anticipation, the list of those who had passed successfully was read. The others were told to fall out and told they could go. Business began immediately for the 'new catch,' or in cadet parlance, for the 'plebes.'"[5]

When the examinations ended on June 14, only 69 of the 130 nominees had gained admittance. Four more passed but were not admitted because they were alternates for whom no vacancies existed. Three others were authorized a delay until August 28 due to sickness or some other unavoidable cause. The medical board rejected five for reasons not specified. One man passed the medical examination and then did not bother to take the academic tests since there was no vacancy open to him. Of twenty-four rejected by the academic board, about half fell short in arithmetic, while the rest failed in grammar, reading, writing, or orthography. Few failed history or geography. Another twenty-four inexplicably failed to report to West Point at the appointed time.[6]

Young easily passed the medical examination and all the academic tests. Not so his two African American colleagues, however, who Young had surely hoped would be his classmates. The three probably roomed together during examination week. The medical board rejected Robert S. Wilkinson, an African American nominee from South Carolina, for unknown reasons. Daniel C. Sugg, from North Carolina, ran afoul of the examination in arithmetic, geography, and history. These two were the first of a number of blacks who made an appearance while Young was at the academy and either failed the entrance examinations or flunked out after one semester.[7]

Plebe Year

Young began his stint at the academy with seventy-five other new cadets. In addition to the sixty-eight cadets who passed the entrance exam with him, there were five cadets who had been turned back from the previous year and two foreign cadets. On June 15, 1884, academy officials administered the oath of office and admitted the young men as "conditional cadets." This oath required Young to "serve in the army of the U.S. for 8 years (4 years after graduation) unless sooner discharged by competent authority." Should he survive the summer encampment, successfully complete the first academic semester, and pass his exams in January 1885, he would no longer carry the conditional classification and would receive a warrant as a cadet.[8]

An 1888 publication on West Point described the academy as follows: "A more healthy situation could not have been found, and in point of beauty it is unsurpassed. . . . West Point, already beautiful by nature, and being the recipient of every possible artistic improvement, promises a treat to the visitor in search of one of the most beautiful places on earth, and to the new cadet a most pleasing place as the scene of his future troubles and pleasures." Young would experience numerous troubles at West Point and enjoy few pleasures, but his excitement surely overmatched his trepidation when he took the oath that sunny day in June.[9]

New cadets endured substantial physical and mental hardships during a grueling first year as fourth classmen, or "plebes." The term *plebe* came from the Latin *plebs*, the common people, who were considered separate from the patricians, or upper classes. When and how this term entered the cadet parlance is unclear, but the use of Roman terms at a military academy was understandable. If a plebe survived his first year of routine hazing, strict discipline, and rigorous academics, the corps accepted him as a full member.

Lassiter described the plebe "brace" required of new cadets: "Once in uniform we all were required to assume and maintain at all times, out of doors, the plebe 'brace': head up, eyes to the front, shoulders well pressed back, stomach sucked up, and hands against the seam of the trousers, palms to the front. In walking, the leg had to be extended so as to straighten the knee in each stride, and the toe depressed so as to bring the weight first on the ball of the foot. All of this may sound very foolish to the uninitiated," Lassiter admitted, "but it is very remarkable, with these posturings and with much calisthenic exercise, how quickly you can, at the pliable age of 17 or 18, take the humps out of backs, convert weak chests into strong ones, and give a boy a fine upright carriage and appearance, and start him on the road to health and strength."[10]

Hazing, also referred to as deviling, had always been a feature at West Point, but in the first half of the 1800s it was mostly limited to harmless pranks practiced during summer camp. It took on a more ominous aspect after the Civil War, encompassing the entire first year and featuring upperclassmen forcing plebes to do exhausting physical exercises, eat or drink unpalatable foods, and generally humiliate themselves. The cause of this growth in hazing is unclear, but it seemed to be connected with the fall in disciplinary standards during the Civil War, when much of the faculty went off to fight, and the postwar attempts to restore discipline by taking away cadet privileges. Whatever the cause, the plebes accepted deviling as a rite of passage, took pride in their ability to endure it, and looked forward to the day when they could dish it out.[11]

By the time Young arrived at West Point, hazing had been brought back under control and was in a lull period. This did not mean life was easy for the plebes, however. Lassiter commented on the methods and reasons for stripping new cadets of their individuality and bringing them all to a common level, noting that "no pains were spared to make us aware of our new complete unimportance in the sphere of things. This latter part of the system was the work of the cadets, the upperclassmen. They felt it to be their inescapable duty to take the new class in hand and imbue it with the proper ideas. The strength of this feeling," he continued, "and the unanimity with which it was acted upon, is really remarkable when you consider that hazing was forbidden and that flagrant hazing, if discovered, was very apt to end in dismissal of the offender from the Academy. As far as the officials of the Academy were concerned, the question would always arise as to where the line should be drawn between hazing and the permissible influence to be exerted by the upper classmen in carrying out the traditional unwritten laws of the Academy."[12]

For a plebe, isolation was the only thing worse than hazing. A new cadet was never allowed to feel like a true part of the corps until he successfully completed his first year and became an upperclassman. In an odd way, plebes welcomed deviling as a relief from this isolation, since the upperclassmen were at least paying some attention to them, even if in a negative way. A plebe's only refuge from the constant pressure of hazing was the support and comradeship of his classmates. For the most part, however, Young, as an African American, was denied this vital refuge.[13]

Plebes learned from the moment they entered West Point that teamwork was the key to survival at the academy. Upperclassmen taught new cadets to win the trust of their classmates and rely heavily on one another. To drive home the lesson, if one plebe made a mistake, all the plebes in his section, squad, or platoon were punished. This was the same sort of teamwork these future leaders would foster in the Regular Army in life-or-death combat situations.

African Americans at West Point

In the nineteenth century, a black cadet at West Point was generally "silenced" or "cut" from the corps as soon as he arrived, denoting that his classmates shunned him and that professors and cadets from the other classes spoke to him only in the line of duty. African Americans were not hazed or deviled in the same manner as white plebes. It is clear from contemporary accounts that Young endured occasional racial slurs, especially during his first year, but for the most part he was ignored and socially isolated.[14]

The terms "silence" and "cut" denoted a treatment dealt to certain members of the Corps of Cadets. This treatment was usually connected with violations of gentlemanly behavior. The earliest recorded use was in 1807, when a cadet was punished by denying him all social intercourse, and any other cadet who did not comply was threatened with the same treatment. It was derived from the code of honor of an officer and gentleman, and violations of the code resulted in the cadet's being ostracized by his fellow cadets. This combined with the traditional pressures of West Point were often enough to cause the cadet to resign. The treatment afforded a black cadet in the nineteenth century was a modified version of this silence.[15]

However, a closer look at the treatment of individual African Americans in the 1800s reveals a more complex picture. Although many have tended to generalize and oversimplify black cadet experience, it varied significantly depending on how long the individual remained at West Point and how he reacted to the rigors of discipline and academics. This treatment also had a great deal to do with the cadet's individual character and temperament and how he dealt with the unique communal pressures of the corps. Cadets who pushed too hard or in the wrong direction were more likely to fail. On the other hand, if he found the right balance he had nearly as good a chance as his white classmates to graduate from West Point.

Between 1870 and 1884, congressmen nominated twenty-two African Americans to West Point, but only nine passed the entrance examination and were admitted as cadets. Prior to Young's arrival, only one had managed to graduate: Henry Ossian Flipper. Another, John Hanks Alexander, had successfully completed one year when Young arrived in 1884. Of those who were unsuccessful, a certain number failed because they could not meet the rigorous academic standards. Still others could not endure the combination of academic stress and social ostracism. Some in desperation sought aid from their congressmen or leaked stories about their unfair treatment to the press, earning the ire of their classmates and the faculty and dooming any chance to graduate.[16]

The first African American to gain admittance to West Point was James Webster Smith, who was appointed by a Republican congressman from South Carolina in 1870. The corps ostracized Smith, and white cadets refused to share the same room in the barracks or the same table in the mess hall. His first year was plagued by open tension and a public fight—an *affaire d'honneur*—that resulted in his being turned back one year. The following year Smith seemed to find a better balance, though the social exclusion and racial slurs persisted.[17]

Smith continued his solitary struggle for the next three years. His loneliness was mitigated in 1873 when another African American,

Henry Flipper from Georgia, joined him. Smith sent a note to Flipper shortly after his arrival in which he implored the latter "to avoid any forward conduct" and not make the same mistakes in dealing with the corps that he had. Of this "sad letter," Flipper later wrote that nothing had "so affected me or influenced my conduct at West Point as its melancholy tone." The two roomed together for the next year until Smith was found deficient in natural and experimental philosophy (physics) in 1874 and dismissed from the academy.[18]

Henry Ossian Flipper

Henry Flipper, who graduated from West Point in 1877, was a truly remarkable man. He left a wealth of information about his time at the academy in his autobiography, *The Colored Cadet at West Point*, published in 1878. "At the hands of the officers of the institution my treatment didn't differ from that of the other cadets at all," he wrote, "and at the hands of the cadets themselves it differed solely 'in the matter of personal public association.' I was never persecuted, or abused, or called by opprobrious epithets in my hearing after the first year. I am told it has been done, but in my presence there has never been anything but proper respect shown me. I have mentioned a number of things done to me by cadets, and I have known the same things to be done to white cadets."[19]

After Flipper graduated, newspapers made a great deal of fuss about his experiences at West Point. Most got the facts wrong, and he felt compelled to set the record straight. About his isolation he wrote: "I must revert to that *Herald's* article just to show how absurd it is to say I never heard the sound of my own voice except in the section-room. I heard it at reveille, at breakfast, dinner, supper roll-calls, at the table, at taps, and at every parade I attended during the day—in all no less than ten or twelve times every single day during the four years. Of course I heard it in other places, as I have explained elsewhere. I have always had somebody to talk to every single day I was at the Academy."[20]

Regarding his loneliness, Flipper wrote that he "was the happiest man in the institution, except when I get brooding over my loneliness, etc. Such moments would come, when it would seem nothing would interest me. When they were gone I was as cheerful and as happy as ever. I learned to hate holidays. At those times the other cadets would go off skating, rowing, or visiting. I had nowhere to go except to walk around the grounds, which I sometimes did. I more often remained in my quarters. At these times the barracks would be deserted and I would get so lonely and melancholy I wouldn't know what to do."[21]

What Flipper seemed to be saying about his own experience at West Point was that it was not altogether different from that of his white classmates. He maintained that he was treated with respect and never abused after his first year, when he was deviled like all the other plebes. The only difference in his treatment was "in the matter of personal public association," meaning the cadets avoided public contact with him. Otherwise, he always had someone to talk to at the academy and was subject to the same bouts of loneliness as the rest of the cadets.

Flipper learned to deal with the pressure, prejudice, and isolation with a combination of composure, self-reliance, intelligence, and humor. According to Thomas Fleming, Flipper applied the theory of nonviolence and proved its power ninety years before Martin Luther King Jr. Above all else, Flipper faced the challenges of West Point himself and did not seek recourse through the newspapers, Congress, or the faculty. In the process, he gradually gained the grudging admiration—or at least the tolerance—of even his most ardent critics within the corps by hard work, patience, and perseverance. Young would learn to follow this example.[22]

Perhaps the most highly publicized account of an African American cadet's failure at West Point was that of Johnson Chestnut Whitaker. Whitaker entered the academy in 1876 from South Carolina and roomed with Flipper for one year until the latter graduated. He tried to follow Flipper's example of responding to ostracism with quiet hard work, but he failed to follow one unwritten rule of the academy: when a white cadet struck him, Whitaker turned him in rather than fighting the cadet himself. The resulting anxiety and added torment from the Corps of Cadets proved too much for Whitaker, especially without Flipper's companionship.[23]

On April 6, 1880, Whitaker failed to report for reveille and was subsequently discovered tied to his bed, bleeding from a beating he claimed had been delivered by several masked men. The superintendent, Maj. Gen. John M. Schofield, immediately started an investigation, and the War Department, aware of the sensitive nature of the incident, sent a Staff Judge Advocate officer from Washington to assist in the inquiry. In the midst of the investigation, which dragged on for months, Whitaker was found deficient in natural and experimental philosophy and dismissed.

Initially the authorities accepted Whitaker's story, but later they concluded he had concocted the assault to divert attention from his academic difficulties. After two additional years of investigations and inquiries, a court-martial convicted Whitaker of perjuring himself and of "conduct unbecoming of an officer and a gentleman." Regardless of whether or not Whitaker was guilty, Pres. Chester A. Arthur's disapproval of the proceedings did not save Whitaker because of his failure in physics. In the meantime, the newspapers and politicians had a field day publicizing the whole affair, and the superintendent was replaced in part due to his perceived mishandling of the incident. In spite of everything, even if Whitaker had followed Flipper's example, his academic difficulties doomed him to failure.[24]

John Hanks Alexander

The African American cadet John Hanks Alexander was already attending West Point when Young arrived in 1884. Alexander entered in 1883, a year after the end of the Whitaker trial, and was faring well at the academy in both academics and discipline, following Flipper's example. Alexander, also from Ohio, was in the class of 1887, and he and Young would have been classmates if Young had been appointed the primary candidate instead of Stamats in 1883. It likely would have made quite a difference in both of their lives.

Although Alexander was doing well his second ("yearling") year at West Point, he still had difficulties. The following passage typifies the day-to-day prejudice he experienced and also illustrates the differences in treatment by his white classmates. The account comes from a memoir by Mark Hersey, class of 1887: "In my yearling year I had for my room mate Bob Howze.[25] . . . While living with Howze, his dominant characteristics of a fire-eating Texan were in evidence. One Saturday afternoon when I was on the area [walking punishment tours], by rare chance our colored classmate, Alexander, was not on the area that day. The skating was good on the Hudson, and as he passed me I offered him my skates and told him where they hung in my alcove."[26]

This was where Alexander's difficulties began with Howze, as Hersey explains: "He went to get them but Bob Howze, who was in confinement, fired him out and he came down empty-handed. As he passed me, I asked him if he did not find the skates, and he said briefly that Howze would not let him have them. When I got off the area I tackled Bob about it and he, with enthusiastic profanity, let me know that no colored man could enter his room in any social way, in fact said that he would never have come to the damned place if he had known he was going to have a nigger for a class mate. We were on official terms for some days thereafter."[27]

Hersey's story illustrates several important points about African Americans at West Point in this era. It supports the generalization that cadets from the South harbored more racial prejudice than those from the North (Howze was from Texas, Hersey from Maine). Howze's actions and "enthusiastic profanity" indicated that Alexander and Young had this type of racism thrown in their faces fairly regularly. Finally, there were cadets like Hersey who were perfectly willing to befriend African American cadets and treat them as equals.

But there is more to the story than this. Hersey notes that Alexander "by rare chance" was not walking punishment tours on the area that day. He seems to intimate that Alexander spent a lot of time on the area, with the implication that this happened thanks to the efforts of cadets like Howze. Alexander did earn, fairly or unfairly, more than his share of demerits, receiving 144 demerits his first year, 147 his second, 171 his third, and 163 his final year. To put this in perspective, only three classmates who survived plebe year with him earned more demerits than he did, four the second, none the third, and three his senior year.[28]

Upperclassmen and faculty officers handed out demerits to new cadets for lesser offenses such as not properly maintaining their uniform, while more serious offenses such as being caught off-limits in a local tavern would earn punishment tours or dismissal.

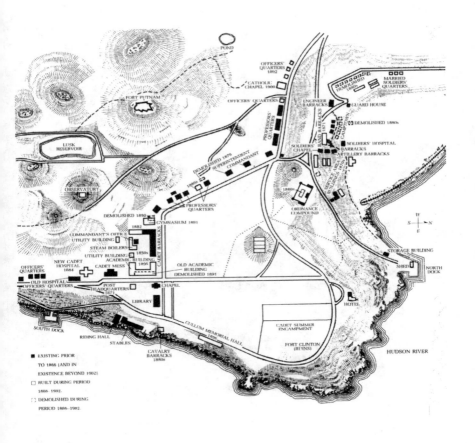

POND

OFFICERS'
QUARTERS
1892

DEMOLISHED

MARRIED
SOLDIERS'
QUARTERS

CATHOLIC
CHAPEL 1900

OFFICERS' QUARTERS

ENGINEER
BARRACKS

GUARD HOUSE

FORT PUTNAM

DEMOLISHED 1880s

PROFESSORS'
QUARTERS

SOLDIERS'
CHAPEL

SOLDIERS' HOSPITAL
BARRACKS
ARTILLERY BARRACKS

LUSK
RESERVOIR

SUPERINTENDENT

DEMOLISHED 1879

COMMANDANT

ORDNANCE
COMPOUND

OBSERVATORY

PROFESSORS'
QUARTERS

W
S — N
E

DEMOLISHED 1890

GYMNASIUM 1891

STORAGE BUILDING

COMMANDANT'S OFFICE
UTILITY BUILDING

STEAM BOILERS

UTILITY BUILDING
ACADEMIC

NEW CADET
HOSPITAL
1884

CADET MESS

ACADEMIC
BUILDING
1895

OFFICERS'
QUARTERS

SHED

NORTH
DOCK

OLD ACADEMIC
BUILDING
DEMOLISHED 1891

OLD HOSPITAL
OFFICERS' QUARTERS

POST
HEADQUARTERS
1871

CHAPEL

LIBRARY

HOTEL

SOUTH DOCK

CULLUM MEMORIAL HALL
1898

RIDING HALL

STABLES

CADET SUMMER
ENCAMPMENT

HUDSON RIVER

CAVALRY
BARRACKS
1880s

FORT CLINTON
(RUINS)

■ EXISTING PRIOR
TO 1866 (AND IN
EXISTENCE BEYOND 1902)

□ BUILT DURING PERIOD
1866–1902.

⬭ DEMOLISHED DURING
PERIOD 1866–1902.

10. Map of West Point, 1866-1902
(Dr. Theodore J. Crackel)

11. Cover from April 21, 1880, *Puck* showing an African American cadet running the gauntlet to get his commission at West Point (Author's collection)

THE CADETS OF TWO COLOURS AT WEST POINT MILITARY ACADEMY.
SHADOWS ATHWART THE PATH OF LOVE.

12. Illustration from British publication *Here and There* (early 1870s) with the caption "The cadets of two colours at West Point Military Academy, Shadows athwart the path of love," showing white cadet and black cadets and their girlfriends (Author's collection)

13. Henry O. Flipper, 1870
(West Point Library Special Collections)

14. John H. Alexander, 1887
(West Point Library Special Collections)

15. Charles Young, 1889
(West Point Library Special Collections)

Cadets who earned an excessive number of demerits also walked punishment tours, which required them to walk back and forth in a central barracks area for a certain number of hours. They did this rain or shine, summer or winter, clad in full dress uniform, and carrying a Cadet Model 1884 Springfield rifle. This tedious and physically demanding work, taking up what precious little free time cadets were granted, was a very effective punishment.

That Hersey risked talking to Alexander while the former was walking punishment tours in the central area of the barracks was itself an act of courage and defiance. White cadets who talked in public to Alexander or Young opened themselves to rebuke and ridicule from the likes of Howze. Beyond that, if the officer of the day had caught Hersey talking to Alexander, the punishment tours already completed would have been rescinded and Hersey might have been awarded additional demerits.

No record exists of how many hours Young walked on the area, but he received a total of 114 demerits during his first six months at West Point. He almost certainly spent, like Alexander, a good number of weekends walking the area. This indicates that the chain of command was holding Young to a standard of discipline comparable to that of his classmates, but it does not prove that he was held to an unfair standard. In the month of August 1884 he received fifty-two demerits, but he was only one of twenty-eight in his plebe class who were allotted an excessive number for the month.[29]

Beast Barracks

Young received the bulk of his demerits during "Beast Barracks," the name for the two summer months the new cadets spent in an encampment. From the completion of June examinations until the end of August, Young and the rest of the cadets remaining at the academy lived in a camp on the Plain. Only three classes remained: the new first class (seniors), the third class (sophomores), and the new plebes. During Beast Barracks, sometimes referred to simply as "Beast," Young and his classmates learned how to behave like new cadets and received their initial military training.[30]

West Point classes were relatively small in the late nineteenth century, with around fifty graduating each year. The following numbers graduated while Young was at West Point: thirty-nine in 1885, seventy-seven in 1886, sixty-four in 1887, forty-four in 1888, and forty-nine in 1889. In 1884, all four classes in the corps totaled fewer than three hundred men when assembled en masse. With one class away on furlough, about two hundred cadets were in the summer encampment. Everyone in each class knew his classmates by name and reputation, and it was extremely difficult to keep a low profile in such an intimate setting. This made the life of a new cadet very demanding and uncomfortable during Beast.[31]

The seniors were in charge of the encampment, with about a half-dozen Regular Army officers from the Tactical Department supervising to ensure that training was conducted properly and that the deviling of the plebes did not get out of hand. The seniors acted as leaders and drillmasters, selected sophomores served as intermediate leaders, and the plebes learned about basic cadet skills. This included what was referred to as practical instruction in the "Schools of the Soldier": artillery and infantry tactics, company and battalion drill, fencing instruction, bayonet exercise, military gymnastics, and the use of small arms.[32]

We have no known firsthand accounts of Young's experiences in Beast Barracks, and Young made no specific mention of it in any known correspondence. A search of the academy's Cullum bi-ographic files revealed not a single mention of plebe summer in the papers of the forty-four graduates from the class of 1888. But West Point official records together with the contemporary accounts of other cadets provide a good picture of Young's experiences and challenges.[33]

The new cadets were initially segregated in the barracks under the supervision of a small number of seniors until they completed their initial processing. The ledger book of Young's classmate Henry Jervey lists the items issued to the new cadets in June 1884:

> Mattress
> Quilt
> Pillow
> Chair
> 2 Sheets

P[illow] case
Flan[ne]l Jacket
Flan[ne]l pants
2 Wh[i]t[e] Jackets
D[res]s shoes
F[orage] Cap
4 p[ai]rs gloves
6 collars
Helmet and trim[min]gs
India Ink
2 Clo[thing] Bags
1 package paper, Shoehorn
Soapdish
2 stocks
D[ress] Hat
6 sets belts
1 Shield (for the dress hat)
Dress Coat:
Tot[al] $76.47.[34]

Young took these items with him when he moved out onto the Plain for the summer encampment.

Out in the tent city on the Plain, Young and the new plebes began a crash course in the schools of the soldier and how to function under pressure. The Plain was a level, grassy area between the barracks and the steep Hudson River embankment that provided room for the encampment and training. Some upperclassmen harassed plebes mercilessly in the process of teaching the former civilians how to salute, march, "brace," and behave like ramrod-straight cadet privates, but most of the upper-class cadets and the Regular Army officers from the Tactical Department who supervised the training were reasonable and led by example.

The routine might have gone like this: the sweating and befuddled plebe was sent off to complete a simple but necessary task. Since he was too afraid to ask directions, he ran off at a double time in the wrong direction. The plebe then became lost and was harassed by any number of upperclassmen along the route. He finally returned to report back to his cadet superior. The plebe was admonished for the poor manner in which he completed the task and sent off on another mission—with similar results.

This went on for weeks, interspersed with endless individual, squad, platoon, company, and battalion drill. All this was done in heavy wool uniforms in summer temperatures reaching the nineties, with a humidity to match. This seemingly pointless routine of harassment under extreme pressure had a purpose, however. It forced Young and his new classmates to learn to think and function under stressful conditions in a controlled environment— skills that could save their lives in combat when the stakes were much higher. Charles Dudley Rhodes, who would become one of Young's classmates the following year, wrote of the behavior of the upperclassmen: "The cadet officers howl and shake their fists in your face, at all times and in all places. If one smiles a thundering voice shouts forth, 'Take that smile off your face, sir.'" The new cadets quickly learned to react to this novel treatment. It was a simple matter of adapt or be eliminated from the corps.[35]

Rhodes added this about life in summer camp: "A fellow has to keep shady and stay in his tent or he will have his life made miserable for him. For instance, I went down to 'C' Co. street, last night to present a report and it took me half an hour to go in and out. In the first place a fellow stopped me and commenced a dialog something like the following: Who are you? What's your name? Where are you from? Who's your predecessor? Know anybody that I know? Why don't you? What you looking at? What tent? What part of the tent? Be more definite! Go and point it out!"[36]

Much of this deviling seemed to be good-natured and akin to college tomfoolery, but the hazing could get mean-spirited and serious, as Rhodes indicated in the following musing: "We have three squad-drills a day. . . . I got the meanest pup Friday that I have seen around here yet. He spotted me, and nothing that I could do was good enough for him. He picked out every fault of mine and totally ignored the other men. He ran into my extended arm, and then accused me of trying to hit him. I'm not bow-legged but he said I was, and made me distort my legs to try to make my knees touch. . . . If I ever have a chance, I'll pay that fellow back!"[37]

Although upperclassmen abused new cadets and hazing became ugly at times, officers of the Tactical Department kept a close watch for abuses, as evidenced in this account by Rhodes: "The [cadet] officers have very playful (?) ways at all times and especially in the mess hall. One of these, in which [John L.] Hayden was engaged in, is to make fellows eat certain things that we don't like. One fellow was through his dinner and left a piece of pie. Hayden ordered him to eat it and when he would not do it, ordered him to report that evening at the office for 2nd Exercise (a punishment). The Supt. of Mess Hall (army officer) overheard him and after an investigation, Hayden was removed from control over us, and [Henry] Jervey put in his place."[38]

Under this kind of indoctrination, Young began accumulating demerits soon after he moved out of the barracks and into the tents on the Plain. The West Point "Register of Delinquencies" lists his infractions in detail, providing a window on some of his troubles. His record began in July, since demerits were not recorded for offenses committed by new cadets during their first thirty days, when they were in a steep learning curve. From July 21 to 31 Young was awarded demerits on seven out of eleven days, whether deserved or undeserved. His "missteps" were as follows:

July 21, Slouching in company street, 7:45 and 8 PM,
3 demerits

July 21, Executing manual carelessly at retreat parade,
2 demerits

July 24, Swinging arms, marching in relief, 7 PM, 1
demerit

July 26, Absent from formation for swimming, 7:30 PM,
3 demerits

July 27, Not covering in file while obliqing, marching to
supper, 2 demerits

July 27, Late at church roll call, 1 demerit

July 29, Making no effort to depress toes in company
street, 6:40 and 6:50 AM, 1 demerit

July 30, Not coming to arms port when speaking to Off[icer of the] Day, 8:45 and 8:50 PM, 2 demerits

July 30, In camp longer than authorized time, 4:16 and 4:34 PM, 3 demerits

July 31, Remaining in camp longer than 20 mins. immediately after reveille, thereby shirking his share of police duty, 3 demerits

July 31, Saluting Off[icer of the] Day with sergeant's Salute 6:50 AM, 2 demerits.[39]

Life only got worse for Young. His demerits for August cover nearly a page of a very large ledger book. He gathered a whopping fifty-two demerits on forty-one individual delinquencies, with infractions earned on all but nine of the thirty-one days in the month. The forty-one breaches broke down as follows: seven times late for formation, twenty occasions of improper marching or weapons handling, and fourteen times where Young was not paying attention to detail. Some of the most amusing in the latter category include three occasions of "gazing about in ranks" during parade or in formation, once caught "talking in ranks," and another time reported "humming on post" at 11:30 p.m. Certainly Young attended the latter offense with a smirk.[40]

Isolation Mitigated

Young survived Beast and moved back into the barracks at the end of August to prepare for the beginning of the academic year on September 1. And he probably survived it mostly alone. It is not clear whether Young roomed with his white classmates in a tent on the Plain during Beast Barracks, nor is it clear if he roomed alone in the barracks during the academic year. Some authors assume he roomed with John Alexander, the other African American at the academy, but this would have gone against the grain of the system at West Point for several reasons.

First, in the highly structured and hierarchical world of West Point, the different cadet classes were strictly segregated. The Corps of Cadets was divided into four companies of between fifty and seventy men each based on height: the tallest in A and D companies and the shortest in B and C companies. This made for uniformly sized marching formations during parades. Within those companies, each a mix of all four classes, plebes roomed with plebes, third classmen with third classmen, and so on. Upperclassmen never roomed with plebes, and since Alexander was an upperclassman, under normal conditions he would not have roomed with Young.

Still, earlier accounts revealed that African American plebes at West Point had been mixed with black upperclassmen. This was the case with both Flipper and Alexander, who roomed with African American cadets from other classes because of their color. Alexander certainly encouraged Young to persevere, whether they roomed together or not. Perhaps the shared fate of being social outcasts narrowed the gulf separating plebe and upperclassman.

A second reason why this ran contrary to the system was connected to the purpose of the distinctive treatment meted out to African Americans at West Point in the nineteenth century. The corps silenced and socially isolated black cadets in part to try to pressure them to quit. This was not the official policy of West Point; in fact, superintendents tried many times to quash the silencing and mistreatment of black cadets. But undoubtedly a portion of the corps hoped that social ostracism, combined with the academic and disciplinary challenges of West Point, would cause Young and other African American cadets to lose their resolve. Strong peer pressure forced many to keep silent, and the silent majority among the cadets who went along with this treatment, at least in public, abetted those who actively promoted this racial intolerance.

The system of discipline at West Point, and the upperclassmen who ran the system, were bent on weeding out those without the grit to succeed from the moment a cadet entered the academy to the day he graduated. The prevailing notion in society at the time was that African Americans were inherently inferior to whites. New cadet Charles Rhodes wrote this to his parents when he learned that he would have a black classmate: "With all due regard for the race, I don't think it wise to mix the two races, as they do here—They can't assimilate."[41] In this environment, it was all too easy to label blacks as "unsuitable" and therefore make them candidates for detrimental treatment and exclusion.

Young probably roomed with Alexander during his plebe year, but we have no record to prove this. He may well have roomed with him in the tent city during Beast Barracks also. If he did, it must have made the social ostracism and racial prejudice somewhat easier to endure.

Academic Challenges

During the encampment on the Plain, Young endured strenuous training and endless hazing in the hot summer sun. Beginning in September, a demanding array of academic classes was added to the mix. For him and the other plebes who had survived Beast Barracks, the next test was the first semester of classes.

The course of study at West Point during Young's first semester included five broad areas: mathematics; modern languages; history, geography, and ethics; the tactics of artillery and infantry; and the use of small arms. Integrating algebra, geometry, trigonometry, and surveying, the math instruction represented the most difficult challenge for most new cadets. English was studied the first semester and French and English the second under the Department of Modern Languages. History, geography, and ethics incorporated lectures in ethics and "Universal History." The tactics of artillery and infantry and the use of small arms built upon the skills the plebes had learned during Beast.[42]

Academics were exceedingly difficult and always competitive at the academy. Cadets studied long hours, drilled in the classroom, and justified their answers and reasoning on a chalkboard in front of their teacher and classmates. The departments divided each class into ability groups or sections for each subject. The lower the group or section number, the higher the ability of the cadet in that subject. Cadets were continually tested and reshuffled according to their standings. The top achievers competed for the top position in the lower sections, and those with academic problems struggled to avoid the bottom ranking in the highest section. A cadet who teetered near the bottom, especially around the semiannual examination periods in January and June, flirted with dismissal.

Young's academic performance during his plebe year was mixed.

Though exceptionally gifted in the humanities and languages, he experienced great difficulties in mathematics his first year. After the January 1885 examinations, which marked the end of the first semester, Young ranked in the upper quarter (twenty-second of ninety-one) in English but the bottom quarter (fifty-eighth of seventy-five) in mathematics. These combined with his disciplinary ranking gave him a general order of merit of forty-sixth out of seventy-five in his class who passed the final exam. Twenty-five of his classmates were found deficient in academics, either in mathematics or English, and discharged. Young had survived the first cut. [43]

Two classmates who shared Young's academic struggles were foreign cadets. On February 2, 1884, Congress had approved a joint resolution providing for the instruction of selected cadets from outside the United States. It was thought that these foreign cadets would take home important engineering skills and American military professionalism. The first to take advantage of this act of Congress were Antonio Barrios from Guatemala and José Victor Zavala from Nicaragua, both of whom entered in 1884 with the class of 1888. Both would suffer difficulties akin to Young's in academics and racial prejudice. [44]

During the second semester, Young battled in vain to master mathematics. Although he finished in the upper third (twenty-fifth of seventy-five) in French and in the upper half (thirty-second of seventy-eight) in English, mathematics dragged him under. The Mathematics Department found him deficient after the June 1885 exams, though he was not alone in his failure. Of eighty-one cadets in Young's class who made it to the annual examination in June 1885, seventeen were found deficient in academics, and fifteen of these were deficient in mathematics. [45] The department had a menacing reputation at the academy, and the excessive numbers of cadets failing in mathematics was the subject of a special investigation by the Academic Board of Visitors in 1885. But this was no help to Young. [46]

Young's military career could have ended there, as was the case with eleven of his classmates who were sent home in humiliation on the first available transport. However, the academic board recommended that Young be turned back to join the next plebe class, and he was readmitted in 1885 with the class of 1889. This meant he would have to repeat his entire first year, from Beast Barracks to final examinations.[47]

To be turned back to the next class and repeat a year was not an unusual occurrence at West Point. Young shared this fate with William Graves, James Normoyle, Joseph Leitch, Antonio Barrios, and José Zavala. If a cadet showed promise in academics in general and the academic board judged that he had the character to succeed, he might be given another chance. After all, the academy had already invested a good deal of time, training, and money in these cadets. However, if the cadet showed no academic promise, had an excessive number of demerits, or fell short in the area of discipline, he was generally not given another chance.

It was perhaps at this point, if ever in his West Point career, that Young had a crisis of confidence. A family account detailed an occasion during his first year when Charles lost heart. Arminta felt sympathy for him and "wanted to recall her son," but Gabriel "refused to think of such weakness" and counseled Charles to stay the course. In the end, "the son justified his father's confidence in his son's ability to endure."[48]

Having to repeat his plebe year must have seemed a cruel yet fortunate fate for Young. He had waited two years for admission to West Point, passed the entrance examinations, survived Beast Barracks, endured social ostracism, faced racial insults, and completed January exams, only to fail at mathematics in June. He could have called it quits and caught a train back to Ohio. But this was the first of many occasions where Young chose the more difficult path, as obstacles and adversity only made him more determined to succeed.

4. Plebe Year Again

I have no color prejudices. . . . All I care to know is that
a man is a human being, and that is enough for me;
he can't be any worse.

MARK TWAIN

In the summer of 1885, Charles Young faced the grim prospect
of another Beast Barracks. Ironically, his classmates from the
previous year now served as part of the leadership cadre, deviling
the candidates and helping the senior class run the tent city on the
Plain. As he joined the untested class of 1889, Young knew too well
the ordeal he faced in the coming year.

The academic year after Beast Barracks would be fairly straight-
forward if not easy for Young. There were no surprises, since he had
taken the courses before. Math might be a challenge, but he could
breeze through English and French as he had his first year. Still,
the combination of academics, discipline, and isolation remained a
formidable set of hurdles to overcome.

New Classmates

One invaluable source of information on the class of 1889 turned
up in the letters of Charles Dudley Rhodes. Rhodes, one of Young's
new classmates, wrote his parents frequently about every facet of
cadet life. The letters, valuable because of their sheer number and
depth of description, are full of the minutiae of daily cadet life
covering the entire four-year journey of the class of 1889. Although
Rhodes mentions Young in only a handful of the letters, his musings
provide nearly a day-by-day description of the struggles of Young
and the rest of his classmates.[1]

Rhodes, like Young, was appointed from Ohio, and his views probably represented those of the rank-and-file cadet of the time. The letters are blunt and bigoted at times, influenced by Rhodes's white, middle-class values and the societal norms of the day. Some cadets, and especially those from the South, were more racially prejudiced, while others were more open-minded and progressive. Rhodes's letters serve as a barometer of the mainstream view toward an African American cadet.

Rhodes first mentions Young in a letter to his parents on June 17, 1885: "Did I tell you we have one *colored* candidate from the Carolinas and one who went through last year, will be turned back into our class, on account of being 'found.' 'Found' means found deficient. . . . The 'turn back' is as black as the ace of spades. There is one bright darkey, in the 2nd class, who is going through first rate. The cadets have little to do with them and I don't blame them."[2] Rhodes's "*colored* candidate from the Carolinas" was William Trent Andrews, appointed from South Carolina. The "found" or "turn-back" cadet was his new classmate Charles Young. The "2nd class" cadet was John Alexander, then beginning his third year. Rhodes failed to mention one other African American candidate, William Achilles Hare, perhaps because Hare's complexion was so light that he could pass for a white cadet.

The situation in the summer of 1885 must have seemed oddly familiar to Young. He had started the previous year hoping that two other African American candidates would pass the entrance tests and share with him the challenges of plebe year, but both had failed. In 1885, however, Hare and Andrews passed the entrance examinations and joined the class of 1889. This news must have eased Young's anguish and disappointment at having to face another plebe year. He gained two African American classmates with whom he could share the pressures and prejudice, and, as an added bonus, Hare hailed from Young's home state of Ohio.

The importance of the Ohio connection of a number of cadets in the class of 1889 is difficult to assess but cannot be ignored. In addition to Hare and Rhodes, eight other members of Young's class were born in or appointed from Ohio. Was Rhodes embarrassed or resentful of the fact that Young and Hare shared his home state?

This might help to explain some of the bitterness he later exhibited toward Young in some of his letters. Walter Bethel and Delamere Skerrett, mentioned in Young's Liberia letter as friends, also shared this important Ohio connection. Finally, although Alexander was born and raised in Arkansas, he received his appointed to West Point while attending Oberlin College in Ohio.[3]

In a long letter to John P. Green, Hare offered this first impression of his new classmate William Andrews: "There is one colored cadet among the new ones by the name of Andrews. He is quite a nice young man and is liked by the more intelligent class. He attends strictly to his own business, is rather conservative in conversation, never pushing himself forward in any manner, and all told is a very gentlemanly young man." Hare also mentions Young and Alexander: "I went to church a few Sundays ago and to my astonishment I found that Mr. Alexander and Mr. Young both occupied the same pew and more than that they were the only ones in it. I do not know whether they were placed among the white cadets or not but I noticed that feature of the regulation particularly. It may have been that it just happened that they occupied it together that Sunday, but I think that the pew is theirs. Mr. Alexander is very popular in the corps so I have been informed, but Young the other colored cadet is not as much so as Mr. A[lexander]. They cannot help but recognize the good qualities of Mr. A."

Hare made these remarks to Green less than two weeks after he passed the entrance exam and a week before he and his classmates moved into camp on the Plain. He seemed to know Andrews well but was not yet familiar with Young. It is interesting that Hare's observations were those of an almost disinterested neutral party and that he was content to conceal his color for a time. When he revealed to his classmates that he was African American remains a mystery. Hare also presented some insightful comments about the prejudice he "observed" among his new classmates in his first weeks at West Point: "There is considerable color prejudice among the new cadets and it exists among the Southerners especially. They are continually murmuring when they have to walk beside Andrews and some of them say that they will not do it. . . . This instance is one of many but I think that it should be stopped. They dare not make any demonstrations of their being prejudiced but one can see it in every action they take regarding color."

He also told Green that he nearly came to blows with one southern cadet candidate: "I had quite a time with a Southerner by the name of Hill. None of the boys know that I am colored and I can easily find what their sentiments are. This 'Hill,' several others, and myself were in the shoe-black room and we were talking about some of the boys, when Hill said, that they should not allow niggers in the academy and that they were beasts. I became angry at this and I told him that they should not permit a *rebel* to enter this institution. He also became angry and we were about to have trouble and would have had it not been for the want of time. I am glad to say that he failed and Andrews passed."[4]

These passages underscore several notions about prejudice at West Point in 1885. First, Hare suggests that the candidates, and especially those from the South, came to the academy with "considerable color prejudice"—not unexpectedly, since they represented a slice of American society. Also, he intimates that the candidates "dare not make any demonstrations of their being prejudiced," indicating that the rules at West Point officially discouraged the practice, though this did not prevent cadets from showing it in private. These features of life at the academy were part of Young's everyday existence.

Beast Barracks

As with the previous year, no known records exist of the living arrangements in the tent city during the summer of 1885. It is almost certain, however, that Andrews, Hare, and Young were tent mates, since Rhodes mentioned in his letters that cadets lived three to a tent. Alexander, the only other African American at West Point at the time, was away with the rest of his class on furlough. The three young African Americans from Ohio and South Carolina faced the crucible of Beast Barracks together. The two newest members of this threesome were lucky to have an old hand to advise them on how best to survive, and Young would have worked hard to help them succeed.[5]

Living in a tent nearby was a young man from Wisconsin named Edward F. McGlachlin Jr., another of Young's new classmates.

"CANDIDATES TURN OUT PROMPTLY!"

FIRST CLASS MAGNATER

16. Candidates turning out, 1886, from the July 1887 *Harper's New Monthly Magazine* (Author's collection)

17. First classmen in summer camp, 1886, from the July 1887 *Harper's New Monthly Magazine* (Author's collection)

18. Charles D. Rhodes, 1889
(West Point Library Special Collections)

19. Ink sketch by Charles Rhodes of
mathematics classroom scene in 1885
(West Point Library Special Collections)

20. Ink sketch by Charles Rhodes of
Thanksgiving in the mess hall in 1885
(West Point Library Special Collections)

McGlachlin wrote an unpublished account of his cadet experiences that serves as another valuable source of information on Young and the class of 1889. It was a frank and unpolished description by one of the circle of friends Young mentioned in his Liberia letter. Unfortunately, McGlachlin wrote it many years later and it is not as precise and detailed as Rhodes's letters. But McGlachlin makes up for this with his sense of humor and bluntness.

Here is McGlachlin's report on swimming instruction during Beast Barracks: "There was no legitimate swimming except up the river. We marched up there for instruction and qualification. The lat[t]er consisted of being able to remain in deep water for ten minutes, one need not swim. On the first day I achieved about the only distinction of all my four years by staying in 45 minutes. Those were about the only or at least the longest period of complete freedom that I enjoyed during the camp. After qualification, one could attend swimming or not, as he pleased, and I think that I always pleased, for camp was not a place to be for pleasure. There was at least one man, John Rogers Meigs Taylor, who never could learn to swim."[6]

Young might have had trouble with swimming too, at least during his first plebe year. The record of delinquencies shows he was "absent from formation for swimming" in July 1884 and "late at formation of squad for swimming" the following month. According to McGlachlin's account, this indicated that Young probably did not pass the initial qualification test and had to take additional instruction. It also may indicate that he did not enjoy the lessons very much, and perhaps for good reason. The Hudson River was wide, deep, studded with rocks, and rife with currents on the West Point side. Swimming fatalities among the cadets were not unheard-of.[7]

The only other activity McGlachlin admitted he enjoyed during Beast Barracks was dancing school. Dancing was an important social skill for future officers. "As a boy I had gone to dancing school and so it was not long before I qualified at dancing," McGlachlin recounted, "so I stag-danced a great deal. The teacher and his assistant were a father and son, German civilians. The hour was free from upper classmen. Discipline was lax. I liked best to be 'Bunker' Haan's partner. He was the oldest in the class and very strong."

In his Liberia letter, Young mentions William George Haan as a friend.[8]

McGlachlin was one of the youngest and shortest members of the class of 1889. "When I was sworn in I was two days beyond the legal minimum age [of seventeen] and the youngest in the class," he noted. "I was pretty nearly the smallest too, for I was assigned to 'C' company and was No. 2 in the rear rank of the first set of fours." He added that the only man in his class who was shorter, and hence had the position to his right in the rear rank, was José Zavala, whom he referred to as the "monkey-looking lad from Nicaragua."[9]

The announcement of the death of Gen. Ulysses S. Grant broke the routine of Beast Barracks on July 23, 1885. The black-bordered message lauded Grant as "twice President of the United States, the Defender of the Union, the victorious leader of our soldiers . . . strong in spirit, patient in suffering, brave in death." On August 5 the corps crossed the Hudson to Garrison to salute Grant's passing funeral train as guns on the South Wharf fired a seventeen-gun salute. On August 7 the corps paraded in front of the superintendent's quarters at the exact time the funeral procession began in New York City. Thirteen guns fired at dawn that day, and they continued to fire at thirty-minute intervals throughout the day until dusk, when the battery fired a national salute of thirty-eight guns.[10]

Hazing and Demerits

For Young and his classmates, hazing, deviling, and demerits went hand in hand during Beast Barracks. "In camp the only time I had to be homesick was during nights on guard, particularly on post," remarked McGlachlin. "It was sometimes extremely dark and the dogs howled across the river and I was so lonesome that I almost welcomed the corporal and the sergeant and the officer of the guard and the officer of the day. Previous to our coming hazing had been pretty bad and serious things had happened to plebes on post. That was all over until the condition arose again a few years later."[11]

These observations offer two insights into Young's everyday life. First, the severity of hazing was at a low point during Young's two years as a plebe. Hazing was severe in the years after the Civil War, but the superintendents and commandants had brought it under control by the 1880s. The other item worth noting is McGlachlin's comment that the only time he felt homesick was while on guard duty. West Point purposely filled the life of a plebe with activities requiring the new cadet to think and react all of the time. This left little time for Young to feel either homesick or sorry for himself.

The degree of difficulty experienced by new cadets depended upon how they reacted to the indoctrination dealt out by the upperclassmen. As Young's classmate William Lassiter explained, "I think it may be said that we got much or little attention depending upon how many physical and mental idiosyncrasies we exhibited to our mentors, and how gracefully we took their ministrations. As I was a fairly well set-up boy to start with, and as the stunts that I was made to perform were mainly humorous and I was able to see their funny side, I came off fairly well. As a matter of fact I can't remember that any boy received treatment damaging to body or necessarily to spirit."[12]

Aside from Rhodes's infrequent references to Young in his letters and the McGlachlin and Lassiter narratives, the only window into the day-to-day lives of Young and his black classmates is the record of their demerits during Beast Barracks. Young was awarded nearly the same number of demerits in his second summer camp at West Point as during his first. His total of seventy demerits from June to August was nearly the same as the sixty-eight he earned his first year. Of his African American classmates, Andrews was never in trouble with demerits, while Hare eventually had difficulties with discipline.[13]

John J. Pershing, class of 1886, might have awarded some of these demerits. A senior during Young's second year, Pershing was notorious for handing out demerits and hazing plebes during summer camp. "We have an awful mean captain and I hope he may be removed before long and a new man appointed," Rhodes wrote of Pershing. "Besides ordering us around like cattle, he swears at us something that I have not heard yet from our other officers. None of the old cadets like him as they have confessed to us and he is an exceedingly unpopular man. He reminds me of a perfect 'toady'— or, as they call it here, a 'boot-lick.' He turned me out yesterday night in the middle of washing my face and made me bundle on my jacket and hat, and go out and pick up two or three matches and minute pieces of paper in front of my tent."[14]

Lassiter noted that the second-year cadets—"the fellows who had just ceased being plebes themselves"—were the hardest on them, whereas the seniors were more distant and looked down on the plebes from afar. But Lassiter, like the rest of the plebes, was wary of Pershing: "Pershing was a first classman when I entered, and was the senior cadet officer of the Corps. Him we looked up to with awe, and, when we passed his tent, our 'brace' was something fearful to behold."[15]

Class Rush

The end of Beast Barracks and the encampment on the Plain was traditionally marked with the return of the new third-year cadets from summer furlough. Cadets remained at West Point until graduation with only a single ten-week furlough from the academy. That break came after the cadets had been confined to the academy grounds for two years. Rhodes described the chaotic return: "Yesterday, the 2nd Class came home from furlough, and hundreds of 'cits' [citizens] came to see the meeting, a time honored custom here. The 'Supe' had forbidden it but the cadets were determined to have it anyhow. They formed in one long line on the plain, and patiently waited for the steamer that was to bring the furlough-men, who had rendezvoused in New York. Presently it was heard, and soon afterwards a black mass of men appeared on the brow of the hill, hurrying forward towards camp."

Rhodes continued: "A signal was given and the two classes rushed at each other, fully an eighth of a mile apart, whooping, shouting, and throwing up their caps. Every fellow seized and hugged some other fellow, and all were swallowed up in a dense mass of dust." John Alexander would have been among the returning throng, though it is unknown whether he took part in the class rush and was "seized and hugged" like his classmates.[16]

As part of the class rush, three classes at the academy waited for the appearance of the "furloughmen" on the day they were scheduled to return. When the latter appeared on the Plain, the seniors rushed out to meet them, throwing hats in the air, tearing uniforms, and venting pent-up energy. Tactical officers tried to control the chaos, but they never succeeded in preventing the rush. It was fun, one of the few occasions when the cadets would let themselves go completely out of control, and the corps was loath to give up the tradition.

Maj. Gen. Wesley Merritt, appointed superintendent in 1882 in the wake of the Whitaker scandal, considered the class rush an example of poor discipline. Merritt, a graduate of the class of 1860, had commanded a cavalry division in the Civil War and had been brevetted for gallantry in every grade from major to major general. Though still a colonel of cavalry in the Regular Army, he was permitted to use his brevet major general rank for ceremony, since West Point was a mixed command. A stickler for military courtesy and discipline, he was determined to end the class rush forever, much to the consternation of the cadets. He would succeed in this the following summer.

First Semester

Charles Young, William Hare, and William Andrews survived Beast and moved into the barracks on August 29, 1885, the day after the class rush. Having endured the first test, they now faced the academic year, with demanding classes added to the pressures of plebe life. Young knew what to expect, and if he could master math this second time around he would have little difficulty with the other challenges of the academic year.

There are no known details of the living arrangements of the four African Americans during the first academic semester of the year. Since cadets slept two to a room, Hare and Andrews likely bunked in one room and Young and Alexander in another. Concerning the barracks arrangements, Rhodes complained that he and another cadet were on guard duty at the time and as a consequence "got left on the choice of rooms in the barracks and most of the desirable ones were taken when we applied." Since cadets had some choice of rooms and roommates, and assuming Young and Alexander shared the same room the previous year, it is likely that did so this year also. [17]

According to a January 1886 listing of the battalion organization, Young belonged to Company B, commanded by Cadet Capt. Mason M. Patrick. Patrick went on to graduate second in his class and enjoyed a distinguished career in the Corps of Engineers. Patrick's company strength was sixty-three cadets, including himself, four lieutenants, a first sergeant, four sergeants, five corporals, and forty-eight privates. The other three companies in the battalion of cadets were of similar strength.[18]

It is instructive to examine who was assigned with Young to Company B. The only two upperclassmen he ever considered friends were in this company: John Alexander, class of 1887, and Malvern-Hill Barnum, class of 1886, the latter one of only two non-classmates mentioned by Young in his Liberia letter. Alexander's role has already been discussed in some detail, but no details are known about the relationship between Barnum and Young.[19]

Malvern-Hill Barnum came by his name in an unusual way. His father was Maj. Gen. Henry A. Barnum, a Civil War hero twice wounded and awarded the Medal of Honor for gallantry in battle at Chattanooga. The elder Barnum suffered his first wound at the Battle of Malvern Hill, where he was left for dead, captured, and exchanged, surviving what should have been a mortal wound. He named his second son after the battle.[20]

Barnum's later service with African American units leaves little doubt about the reason for the connection between himself and Young. During World War I, Barnum commanded a brigade of the African American Ninety-second Division and once stated: "It would not be in accordance with the policy of our Country to close to the colored man the door of opportunity to become officers, and to rise as high as their merit will permit." The two must have had a positive relationship at West Point.[21]

A closer look at Young's classmates in Company B reveals an even more compelling story. Among those classmates were five of the ten members of the class of 1889 whom he considered friends: Ralph Harrison, James Lamblin, James Schermerhorn, Delamere Skerrett, and Frank Webster. Harry Lee, Joseph Monty, and William Wood, the three other members of the class in Company B, did not survive the semester. Formative relationships must have developed with these two upperclassmen and five classmates as they struggled and survived together in the same barracks. The plebes, especially, learned to live with and depend upon each other during this difficult year.[22]

Young established a lasting bond with James Schermerhorn. This friendship must have formed quickly, since Schermerhorn's cadet career was very brief; he resigned on March 15, 1886, barely into his second semester. The death of his father caused him to resign and return to Hudson, Michigan, to run the family newspaper, the *Hudson Gazette*. Schermerhorn later moved to Detroit to found the *Times*. Schermerhorn, Skerrett, and Alexander Piper were Young's closest white friends at West Point.[23]

On the academic side of cadet life, Young overcame his difficulties in mathematics the way he faced all future challenges: through single-minded perseverance. As it turned out, this was perhaps his easiest academic year. His two African American classmates, however, had a more difficult time. When the January 1886 semiannual examinations ended, Young stood in the upper one-fourth in general order of merit. He finished seventeenth out of seventy-seven overall, with thirteen of his classmates declared deficient. He sailed through English easily, ranking twelfth out of eighty-four, with six found deficient. In math he placed a respectable twenty-fourth out of seventy-eight, with twelve found deficient. Andrews failed math, while Hare fell short in math, English, and discipline.[24]

Rhodes made no note of the two African Americans being found deficient, though he did mention by name two other white classmates. "Thirteen of our class were 'found,'" he lamented. "There were some pretty sad sights and shaky voices when we bade our classmates good-bye, on Friday and Saturday." It is doubtful that many of the class of 1889 besides Young noted the loss of Andrews and Hare.[25]

Rhodes did complain, however, about his own class standing relative to Young. His January 25, 1886, letter was an embittered apology to his parents for a class standing of nineteenth, two positions behind Young. He grumbled: "There are three turn-backs above me: Graves, a fellow from Texas; Barrios, the son of the late Guatamala [*sic*] President; and Mr. Young, the negro cadet from Ohio. The latter is on the downward path and won't be above me more than a week."[26]

Those conditional cadets who survived the first grueling semester at West Point received their cadet warrants. This changed their status significantly. On February 7, 1886, Rhodes reported that "the 4th Class received their warrants yesterday and were sworn in for 8 years. We are now U.S. officers and no longer what is called 'conditionalettes.' Full-fledged cadets!!!"[27]

Ironically, cadet candidates who failed after one semester at West Point had to pay for their trip home out of their own pockets. This after the academy deducted all of their debits from a second lieutenant's meager half-pay.

Free Time and Sports

Cadets found ways to entertain and distract themselves from the challenges of the course work and isolation at the academy. Young and his classmates had precious little free time, but they put to good use the little they had. Some found places to pass their quiet time with music and reading. Others organized sports activities, with the academy's encouragement. The cadets also planned dances and shows, many of which caught on and became traditional.

One such tradition was the celebration of "100th Night," which marked 100 days until graduation in June. The first recorded 100th Night Show was held in 1884.[28] Rhodes, who served as an usher for the event in 1886, took special delight at the butt of one joke: "Pershing is the First Captain, a tall, dignified, self-possessed fellow. His part on the program was a hoax. He came there with his 'spoon' [date], and knew nothing about it. We ushers were instructed to give him a prominent seat. When his part on the program was reached, the Grand Mogul announced it. Pershing got white around the mouth, and in response to cheers and repeated encores, had to get up, very much embarrassed, and make a speech. He is so rarely disconcerted that the audience fully appreciated the joke."[29]

Another feature of cadet life that offered a break from the tedium of classes was athletics. In 1885, West Point had hired a civilian named Herman J. Koehler as head of the new Physical Education Department. Also known as the Master of the Sword, Koehler was affectionately nicknamed "Squaredeal" by the cadets, and he reorganized the gymnastic, fencing, and swimming instruction at the academy. He later contributed much to the calisthenics used with the third and fourth classes and also started a comprehensive program of physical education and intramural athletics.[30]

But most of the expansion of West Point sports came in later years. According to McGlachlin, there were no organized athletics while they were cadets, and only plebes were required to attend "gymnasium." This was conducted in an old academic building, and the modest equipment consisted of "dumb-bells, Indian clubs, a few horses, a couple of parallel bars, a few horizontal bars, two or three trapezes, a pair or two of rings, [and] a series of about ten flying rings." They also took fencing instruction.[31]

One pastime enjoyed by both Rhodes and McGlachlin was baseball. Rhodes first referred to the game in April 1886: "We played some baseball yesterday afternoon and threw off all cadet dignity for the time. The officers stop to watch us and seem to take a good deal of interest in it." Baseball was a fairly new American sport in 1886. Abner Doubleday, a graduate of the class of 1842, was often credited with devising and naming the game at Cooperstown, New York. Perhaps the Doubleday connection was one reason it was played so early at West Point.[32]

While Young was at the academy, cadets played sports in their regular-issue uniforms. Their uniforms were of a looser fit then and allowed more freedom for athletic activities. The only special uniform issued for exercise was for horseback riding. Distinctive light sports clothing did not appear in the general public until the turn of the century, but it made an appearance at West Point in 1890. That year, on a challenge from the Naval Academy, West Point hastily formed a football team. To distinguish the players from their opponents, a special football uniform was adopted consisting of a white turtleneck sweater marked with "USMA," football trousers, long black socks, and striped stocking caps. The first Army-Navy football game was played in this uniform in 1890, one year after Young graduated, so they probably played the game while he was there.[33]

McGlachlin also remembered spending some of his idle hours with Young at the piano in the Dialectic Hall. This hall was used by the Dialectic Society for organized debating and doubled as a cadet lounge. "My off-hours in barracks were spent in the Dialectic Hall, which was a refuge for plebes, a bare, ill-kept and uncomfortable place with a piano and a few newspapers," McGlachlin recalled. "There Negro Young would often play to me on the piano. I had been brought up to think that Negros were pretty angelic and he and I were always friendly. But there entered with us two or three other Negros and they had made such an impression on me that Young and I were never familiar."[34]

This passage reveals a great deal about McGlachlin. He came from the small town of Stevens Point, Wisconsin, and may well have never met a black man before. According to the description, they were on friendly but not familiar terms. McGlachlin explained that a closer friendship did not develop because of his adverse reaction to the two other African American cadets who entered in the summer of 1885. This must have been a reference to Andrews and Hare, but what they did to make a negative impression on McGlachlin is a mystery.

It is remarkable that McGlachlin refused to go along with the majority of the corps who cut and socially isolated Young. It must have taken a great deal of courage to spend time socially with Young and perhaps risk his own ostracism. The answer might lie in McGlachlin's independent streak. He did not always follow the crowd when it came to what he considered important matters.

McGlachlin gave this explanation for refusing to go along with a class stunt that might have resulted in punishment, which could have kept him from seeing his visiting mother and sister: "So I had to decide whether to do as my class did and disappoint them and myself, or keep silent and perhaps be ostracized by my class as a punishment. The class did hurrah [at the furlough rush] and I did keep silent. I visited with my mother and sister. No one paid any attention to my insurgency."[35]

McGlachlin elaborated on his tendency not to go along with the crowd: "On many other occasions in my life I have acted independently and never had reason to be sorry. The crowd is more often wrong than the minority. It is wise enough to run along with the majority or with popular opinion in matters that are not of much importance, but it is dangerous to acquiesce in anything that smacks of prejudice or emotion." This principle gave McGlachlin license and courage to spend time socially with Young.[36]

Second Semester

So Young dealt with the familiar trials of the second semester of plebe year without the companionship of Hare and Andrews. Although he likely roomed with Alexander, it was not the same as having two classmates who shared the same curriculum and the rigors of plebe life. It was preferable to being alone, however, and though Alexander was an upperclassman, he was able to assist Young in course work, pass on survival skills, and counsel patience.

In addition to the graded subjects of math, English, and French, Young received training in ethics, artillery and infantry tactics, and the use of small arms. McGlachlin had these uncomplimentary remarks about the ethics instructor, who was also the Protestant chaplain: "The Chaplain was [William E.] Postlethwaite,—'Pocey' to us. He conducted lectures in 'ethics.' He was grossly fat, his cheeks hung down in jowls, he was pot-bellied, the back of his neck hung over his collar, he was bald, he wore Lord Dundreary whiskers, he screwed his mouth and face in talking. He lingered affectionately on the dirty subjects that he thought must be treated in his lectures. His sermons at chapel were mostly uninteresting; when they were otherwise, we thought he had stolen them."[37]

Young worked hard the second semester and finished math in the upper half of his class, falling from the previous semester to thirty-first out of sixty-five. Nine of his classmates fell victim to the final exam on June 1, 1886, and were found deficient. Rhodes, who finished one position ahead of Young, wrote that "the examination was a scorcher—Heretofore the fourth class has been examined in each branch as soon as the study of it was finished. We were examined in all—Geometry, Trigonometry, and Analytics, in a bunch. The battle lasted six hours exactly and when I got through I felt as if a great load were off my shoulders. Some poor fellows are afraid they are 'found' on what they did today."[38]

Young ranked near the upper tenth of those who passed English, finishing eighth of seventy-two. In French he finished nearly the same, at eighth of seventy-one who achieved a passing grade. Two of his classmates failed English and three French. Rhodes finished thirteenth and twenty-first in English and French, respectively. It must have rankled Rhodes to finish behind Young in these two subjects, though he finished higher overall due to other considerations.

Young earned about as many demerits in his second plebe year as in his first, with 113 in the first semester but only 13 in the second. The total of 126 demerits for the year ranked the third highest for those who successfully completed the year. Only McGlachlin, with 143, and José Zavala, with 216, earned more than he and passed. McGlachlin noted that he had "more demerits than any one who survived, except our Negro classmate Young." He was mistaken.

This high number of demerits caused Young's overall order-of-merit ranking to slide. Young's rank, which combined his results in math, English, French, and discipline, fell to thirty-fourth of sixty-three. Rhodes finished well ahead of him at nineteenth, mainly because he earned only four demerits for the year. McGlachlin finished forty-sixth, also because of his high demerit count. Still, Young finished just below the center of mass of his class and was never in danger of failing academically. Eleven of his classmates were found deficient, and one of these was turned back to repeat his plebe year. [39]

Mark Twain Visits

West Point held a fascination for Samuel Langhorne Clemens, better known as Mark Twain, who made at least ten visits to the academy in the late 1800s from his home in nearby Connecticut. Twain enjoyed the pomp and ceremony of West Point and delighted the cadets with stories, jokes, and speeches. During these visits he met with the cadets in small groups, mixed with the superintendent and faculty, and performed for the entire corps. He even made illegal use of the academy printing press to print one of his early books. Twain visited West Point four times prior to 1884 and three times while Young was there. [40]

General Merritt, who arrived after Twain's fourth visit in 1882, wrote in March 1886: "There is a great desire on the part of the Corps of Cadets and the Army people stationed at the Post to have you lecture at West Point. Can you gratify the wish?" Twain responded that he would visit the following month. West Point Circular number 8, dated April 2, 1886, read: "Mr. Samuel L. Clemens (Mark Twain) will deliver a lecture in the Cadet Mess Hall tomorrow (Saturday) evening at 8 o'clock. The officers, ladies and residents of the post are invited to attend."[41]

The *Army and Navy Journal* described Twain's program: "When Mr. Clemens entered the hall at 8 o'clock he was warmly greeted. . . . After music the lecturer was introduced and gave a selection from Huckleberry Finn, illustrating Huck's interview with the escaped slave regarding the wisdom of Solomon [chapter 14]. The Chapter on German Genders was very funny. Meeting an American girl in a foreign restaurant and Cure for Stammering were next given. The evening's entertainment was ended with the Jumping Frog. The good hits were all generously and vigorously applauded, and it is safe to say that no lecturer ever had a more appreciative audience."[42]

This would have been a command performance for the corps. Cadets would have been assembled and marched to the mess hall for the program if they was not sick or on guard duty, as Rhodes was that night, so we can assume that Young was in the audience listening to Twain recite Huck's conversation with his runaway slave friend, Jim. How odd this moment must have been for Young and his white classmates. Young and Alexander, the only African Americans in the audience, must have been the object of quiet snickers and stolen glances when Twain drawled the slave-era vernacular attributed to Jim.

What strikes the present-day reader of *Huck Finn* is the repeated use of the word "nigger," but since the story was set in the antebellum South, it would be odd if the word was not used. Young certainly heard it used often enough. A close reading of Twain's dialogue between Huck and Jim reveals his satiric intent and use of irony. The discussion and arguments show Jim to be a moral and courageous man with firm ideas and a clear conscience. Twain used the dialogue to cause the reader to feel respect for Jim and sympathy for his plight. Twain was anything but a racist and once commented, "Where prejudice exists it always discolors our thoughts."

Twain made a second visit to West Point in 1886 at General Merritt's invitation, staying as the superintendent's guest from May 5 to 7, 1886. Little is known about the visit, and nothing is recorded about the visit, and nothing is recorded about the stories he may have told. Merritt reportedly encouraged Twain to mix informally with the cadets. The cadets wanted to demonstrate infantry, cavalry, and artillery drill, but this was put off for unknown reasons until a later visit. Twain used the this trip to gather background information for *A Connecticut Yankee in King Arthur's Court*, which he was then writing.[43]

Recognition and Furlough

At the end of a successful first year, the upper three classes acknowledged the plebes as full members of the corps. Following graduation parade, upperclassmen who hours before had mercilessly hazed plebes ceremoniously extended their hands in recognition and called them by their given names. Prior to this, plebes had been referred to as "Mister" or "Sir."

McGlachlin observed that the second-year cadet toughest on him his plebe year was the first upperclassman to offer his hand after the graduation parade: "The 'yearling' who rode me the hardest was George Burr. Red-headed and spunky, he was never abusive, but was hard and tough. I thought I hated him, but a year later he was the first upper-classman to shake my hand when I in turn became a yearling."[44] Rhodes also noted the miraculous transformation: "Oh how delightful the change is. The upper classmen threat us like equals and one of the most fierce (formerly) today shouted 'Hello fellow!' And they are quite ready and willing to instruct us 'Corps' [Rhodes had been made a corporal] in our new duties. It is the greatest change I ever experienced. One day treated as an outcast and the next day leading the battalion from dinner as I did today."[45]

No known firsthand account exists of Young's thoughts and experiences after recognition. Although he surely marched in the graduation parade after his second plebe year, it is unlikely that any upperclassmen shook his hand or called him Charles or Young, aside from John Alexander. For that matter, neither did many of his classmates, aside perhaps from his small circle of friends. But Young's hard-won success after two years must have been a satisfying personal victory, and one that he would soon celebrate with his family.

Young and nine of his classmates took a ten-week furlough over the summer of 1886. Normally, cadets went home upon successfully completing their second year at the academy, but the cadets in Young's class who had been held back a year went home at this time rather than with the rest of their class a year later. West Point Order number 94, dated June 14, 1886, stated the following: "paragraph 87 Academic Regulations, leave of absence from 1 o'clock PM tomorrow until 2 o'clock PM August 28 1886 is hereby granted the following named cadets of the Military Academy: Eli A. Helmick and Charles Young."[46]

Young spent at least part of his furlough in Ohio with his mother and father. At some point during his two years at West Point, Young's parents moved to Zanesville, Ohio, so he spent some of his time there. The *Ripley Bee and Times* revealed at least one visit to his old hometown during Young's furlough. The following announcement appeared in the "Local Matters" section on June 30: "Cadet Charles Young, of West Point, is visiting friends, here." Among those he called on were likely his chief mentor, John Parker, and J. C. Shumaker and his former colleagues at the school where he used to teach.[47]

It appears from this announcement that Young traveled to Ripley as a man of some notoriety. The average visitor would not have had the event noted in the local newspaper, and it was probably far less likely for an ordinary black man to be so mentioned. This indicates that Young enjoyed status and some measure of fame as one of only two African Americans attending West Point in 1886. He must have cut quite a fine figure visiting the town in his dashing cadet uniform.

The furlough had one other remarkable consequence. The month of July 1886, when he was absent from West Point, was the first month since entering the academy in June 1884 that Young earned no demerits.[48]

As he neared the end of his furlough that August, Young began to prepare for his return to West Point. In addition to the practical preparations for the train trip to the East Coast, he needed to steel himself mentally. He had spent more than two months among family and friends who treated him like a conquering hero, but upon his return to the academy he would once more face isolation and intolerance. For Young it might have been a more difficult departure than two years earlier, knowing full well what he faced upon his return.

5. Yearling Upperclassman

In this world a man must either be anvil or hammer.

HENRY WADSWORTH LONGFELLOW

Young's third year at West Point had a far different significance for Young than it did for his white classmates. He had survived two long, lonely years as a plebe. Unlike his classmates, who began the academic year as newly recognized and accepted members of the Corps of Cadets, he was still largely isolated from most of his fellow cadets.

Young also had a new year of academic challenges ahead of him. The previous year had been easier than his first, since the fields of study had been the same. But his success the previous year could not guarantee future success. Young faced in the coming year the demanding ordeal of classes in French, drawing, and mathematics.

Yearlings

A West Point cadet's third-class ("yearling") year was a watershed event. The term *yearling* commonly refers to an animal in the second year of its life and emphasizes youth and inexperience. On the one hand, the cadet had survived his first year of grueling academics, demanding physical instruction, and rigid discipline. On the other hand, he was only half a step away from being a plebe and was not yet ready for serious leadership responsibility.

Young had struggled since 1884 to earn his yearling privileges, but the meaning of the year for him was significantly different from that for his white classmates. Though no longer bedeviled as a plebe, he was not given the same acceptance as his classmates. He occupied a gray area, neither totally accepted nor completely ostracized. It might have been easier for him to handle being looked down upon along with his classmates as a lowly plebe than to be isolated and socially ignored as the lone African American yearling.

Had he not been away on furlough, Young would have spent the summer with the rest of his classmates in the encampment, which was called Camp Hancock that year. The lucky among the class of 1889 were made corporals and given minor leadership responsibilities. Charles Rhodes and eighteen of his classmates were awarded chevrons to wear on their lower sleeves after the June 1886 graduation parade. The chain of command assigned the new corporals minor responsibilities, such as corporal of the guard or "left guide" during parades, and a select few were appointed as first-line supervisors over the new plebes.[1]

But corporal stripes were easier to lose than they were to earn. In a July 1886 letter to his parents, Rhodes lamented that he had lost his chevrons for mistreating a plebe. According to Rhodes, he and a corporal classmate were trying to cure a plebe of his habit of "giggling when making reports" and made him stand in the corner of the tent until he could control himself. 2nd Lt. Francis J. A. Darr, a member of the Department of Tactics assigned to supervise the encampment, happened upon the scene and reported the two yearlings for "giving unauthorized punishment to a new cadet." As a reprimand, Rhodes and his classmate were busted to cadet private. This incident illustrated both the mild degree of hazing and the close supervision of the tactical officers.[2]

Rhodes was not the only one to lose his stripes during the year. Young's friend Alexander Piper, along with another classmate named Ben Johnson, lost theirs during the second semester. Piper was among those whom Young mentioned in his Liberia letter and would become one of his closest white cadet friends. Rhodes gave this account: "Piper and Johnson have lost their chevrons. Poor fellows. I know how to feel for them. Johnson lost his for general carelessness in the matter of demerits, having received several reports for smoking lately." Rhodes detailed Piper's "bust": "You know we are allowed to go on an officer's porch, ring the bell, and deliver messages, but are supposed not to take advantage of the permission to talk at length. Well, Piper had been walking with a young lady friend of ours, a Miss Underhill of N.Y., and upon taking her to the door, Mrs. Lieut. Goethals came out and requested Piper to take some notes (invitations to tea) back to barracks for her. She went in to get them and meanwhile Piper had to wait, the young lady also waiting. While thus engaged, Lieut. Price passed. The next day the report came out against Piper, 'loitering on the porch of an officer's quarters.'"[3]

For the yearlings, corporal chevrons were highly sought-after status symbols. Leadership positions were given as a reward for high class standing and a sterling disciplinary record. At the end of the summer encampment, the existing appointments of corporals in the class of 1889 were revoked and a new batch of twenty-one was appointed for the coming academic year. Rhodes's name was not on the list, nor was Young's. Young never wore chevrons while attending West Point, mainly due to his grades and demerits, but also because this would have put him in a position of authority over white cadets.[4]

There were others who never wore chevrons, among them Young's Dialectic Hall companion Edward McGlachlin. McGlachlin was philosophic about the matter: "I managed to squeak through the June exams, skirting danger in discipline. Needless to say, I was not rewarded with any chevrons. I never did wear chevrons, but during my yearling year did crave them slightly. During that year my conduct was pretty good and in the Spring I braced a good deal. Quite a number recommended me, I heard, but the authorities could not overlook my plebe record. After that I never coveted them."[5]

Another member of the class of 1889 who never wore stripes and was mentioned in Young's Liberia letter was Frank Daniel Webster. Nicknamed "Dannie" by his classmates, Webster also shared Young's struggles with academics during his years at West Point. They probably toiled together in the lower-section classrooms, since both had difficulties with math and science. Webster grew up in Rolla, Missouri, and attended the University of Missouri School of Mines. He had the distinction of being one of the few who attended both the U.S. Naval Academy and the U.S. Military Academy. He had entered Annapolis in 1882 at the age of sixteen and was a midshipman until 1884. After a year's break, he entered West Point in 1885 as a member of the class of 1889.[6]

Last Rush

The return of the furloughmen at 2 p.m. on August 28, 1886, signaled the end of the summer encampment at Camp Hancock and the beginning of the academic year. Young and the handful of other turnback yearlings of the class of 1889 returned with the new third-year men of the class of 1888—Young's original class. Although they probably traveled downriver together by ferry, Young's small yearling group did not participate in the class rush. As it turned out, it was probably wise of them not to do so.

Unknown to the returning furloughmen, General Merritt had ordered the new senior class not to take part in the rush. "The 'Supe,' as you know, has been cutting down our privileges for the last four years, until we can hardly turn around," wrote Rhodes to his parents. "Well, the last straw that broke the camel's back was that he forbade the meeting with the furlough class. The 1st class held a meeting, at which many projects were discussed and the meeting adjourned without coming to any decision." On August 28, "the first of the furloughmen were seen at the top of the hill; somebody cheered and cried: 'come on fellows' and with a frantic Comanche yell, the whole 1st class (Class of '87) rushed across the sentinels post towards the furlough class (Class of '88), who were running in the opposite direction. They met. I cannot describe the scene. Of course the officer in charge, officer of the day, and officers of the guard rushed down as fast as possible but the 'rush' was over when they arrived."[7]

Rhodes exaggerated when he indicated the whole first class participated in the rush. The actual count, according to the punishment and court-martial orders, was twenty-seven first-class privates and five first-class officers. Still, this was half of the first class, which numbered sixty-four. But the other seventeen officers and fifteen of the cadet privates had better sense and did not participate in the rush.[8]

21. Cadets on horseback in 1887 with Charles Young in the second rank, second from the left (Coleman Collection)

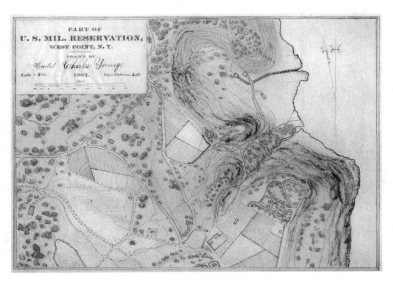

22. Map of West Point by Charles Young, 1887, showing the topography of the north side of the academy grounds (Courtesy of Omega Psi Phi Fraternity Charles Young Collection, National Afro-American Museum and Cultural Center, Wilberforce OH)

23. Drawing of a building by Charles Young, 1887 (Courtesy of Omega Psi Phi Fraternity Charles Young Collection, National Afro-American Museum and Cultural Center, Wilberforce OH)

24. Drawing of Molly Pitcher's carriage by Charles Young, 1887 (Courtesy of Omega Psi Phi Fraternity Charles Young Collection, National Afro-American Museum and Cultural Center, Wilberforce OH)

25. Charcoal sketch of a boathouse by Charles Young, 1887 (Courtesy of Omega Psi Phi Fraternity Charles Young Collection, National Afro-American Museum and Cultural Center, Wilberforce OH)

26. Pencil sketch of Dante by Charles Young, 1887 (Courtesy of Omega Psi Phi Fraternity Charles Young Collection, National Afro-American Museum and Cultural Center, Wilberforce OH)

27. Charcoal sketch of a woman by Charles Young, 1887, with initials "CY" in the lower right corner (Courtesy of Omega Psi Phi Fraternity Charles Young Collection, National Afro-American Museum and Cultural Center, Wilberforce OH)

28. Painting of a woman, probably done by John Alexander, 1886 (Courtesy of Omega Psi Phi Fraternity Charles Young Collection, National Afro-American Museum and Cultural Center, Wilberforce OH)

29. Watercolor of Cadet
Lt. Harry H. Bandholz,
class of 1890, painted by him
in his sketchbook in 1888
(West Point Library
Special Collections)

The officer in charge rounded up all the wrongdoers and marched them back to the barracks. The superintendent was livid with this act of defiance and insubordination and threatened to sack the guilty members of the first class. He took the affair as a personal affront and telegraphed the War Department to ask permission to summarily dismiss half the class of 1887. The War Department wired back a firm negative, well aware that a mass dismissal would provoke a storm of protest in Congress, as well as fearing the consequences of losing half of a class at the academy. But this did not end the affair.[9]

General Merritt insisted that the perpetrators be punished, but he decided that the punishment meted out to the first class be differentiated. He felt that the cadet officers among the first classmen should pay a higher price, since they were in positions of leadership and should have prevented the rush. The superintendent dealt with the twenty-seven cadet privates—those without stripes on their sleeves—through an executive order. They received as punishment "confinement to barracks until next camp" and "tours of extra duty on the area every Saturday during that period." This would have kept them past graduation, but the punishment was later shortened, and Rhodes reported that they were all "free once more" by April 1887.[10]

For the five cadet officers, the commandant, Lt. Col. Henry C. Hasbrouck, convened a general court-martial board consisting of eleven officers on September 4, 1886. The court-martial found every one of the cadet officers guilty of every charge and specification and sentenced them to dismissal. Pres. Grover Cleveland approved the proceedings but mitigated the punishment to reduction in ranks, taking away their chevrons and leadership responsibilities and making them all privates. With this revision in punishment, the cadet privates actually paid a steeper penalty than the cadet officers.[11]

With this act, General Merritt effectively ended the class rush forever, although it survived in a very subdued and tightly orchestrated form in succeeding years. It joined a long list of traditions the cadets felt were taken from them in the name of discipline and good order by the authorities.

Within a year of the famous last class rush, General Merritt was promoted to brigadier general in the Regular Army and replaced as superintendent. Promoted to major general in 1897, he commanded the forces that captured Manila during the Spanish-American War the following year. Although they graduated nearly thirty years apart, Merritt and Young shared one dubious honor in their cadet careers: both had taken five years to graduate from the academy due to being found in mathematics. [12]

First Semester

Young struggled academically as a yearling. At the halfway point he ranked in the top half in order of merit in French, standing twenty-fifth out of fifty-eight, with four of his classmates found deficient. But he registered in the bottom fifth in math, ranking fiftieth out of sixty, with two cadets deficient. Worst of all was his result in drawing, where he finished fifty-seventh of sixty-two. However, none in his class failed drawing in either semester, and cadets were rarely found deficient in this subject. [13]

While Young was having his problems in math and drawing, McGlachlin was overwhelmed with French. He had never heard French spoken before he came to West Point, and he progressed swiftly down the sections until he found himself only one above the "immortal" in the class. *Immortal* was a term reserved for the very last man in the very last section, always in danger of being found. McGlachlin was saved while studying in the library one night when he happened upon a French book on descriptive geometry that proved to be the source of a good many of the problems the professor was handing out. That gave him the advantage he needed, and he made a rapid recovery and finished sixth in French that semester. [14]

Not all of Young's classmates were as lucky getting through midterm examinations. José Zavala resigned and went home to Nicaragua on December 31, 1886, before examinations commenced. Rhodes commented on the other casualties: "Carruthers, Spurgin, Dickey, and Wholley were 'found' out and out—the first and last in French and Spurgin in both Math and French. Clark, W. F. got a turn-back on account of French." After that, things became complicated. "The day after the above was announced, Wholley also got a turn-back also through the influence, it is said, of Professor Bass,"

Rhodes continued. "Old Carruthers, who deserved to get through, is now in Washington and intends to try to get a turn-back, also. He also has been doing quite well although he was in the 'Immortals' in both Math and French. What made it seem the more unjust was that after two or three days Spurgin who was found in both received a turn-back. Spurgin is the son of Capt. S[purgin] our treasurer and commissariat, and the biggest 'goat' in the class."[15]

This letter illustrates another fact of life of West Point at this time. A cadet who was found deficient and slated for dismissal might get another chance if he had an ally on the faculty or political connections in Washington. David Spurgin's father used his contacts in the War Department, and Henry M. Carruthers was trying the same ploy. John H. Wholley at least had the support of Professor Edgar W. Bass, the head of the Mathematics Department, because he had made an effort in the subject. Only William Clark seemed to have earned the "turn-back" on his own merits. Young could never hope for connections in the War Department, but he would later learn to count on a few important allies on the faculty.

Of course, a second chance did not ultimately guarantee success; more often than not it just put off the inevitable. Of the five listed by Rhodes who were found or turned back in January 1887, only two graduated. John Dickey went straight home. Henry Carruthers failed in Washington to curry support and also went home. David Spurgin joined the class of 1890 and hung on until June 1888 before being found again and sent home. Only William Clark and John Wholley, the two who seemed to deserve their turn-backs, graduated in the class of 1890.[16]

There was another reward near the end of the first semester for certain upperclassmen. The semiannual examinations always took place during the first week of January. Most of the cadets were restricted to the post, but a lucky few were able to take a short Christmas leave. In order to qualify for this leave, a cadet had to have "no demerit standing against them for the half year ending December 31." Orders no. 215, dated December 23, 1886, granted six first classmen, seven second classmen, and one third classman leave from December 24 to 27. Young's classmate Eddie T. Winston was the lucky yearling.[17]

Horses, Barracks, and Parades

An array of activities diverted the cadets' attention from the grind of academics and the rigors of discipline. Some events, such as horseback riding, provided practical training for future officers who would be required to ride. Guard duty was a less enjoyable exercise, but it was necessary for the efficient functioning of the academy. And cadets endured parades at the end of each day, punctuated by occasional visits from VIPs.

Equestrian training began for cadets in the fall of their yearling year. Many of the cadets had been exposed to riding before arriving at West Point, but not all. Young was an excellent rider and loved horses, and this was probably the single most important factor in his choice of the cavalry branch after graduation. His time on horseback in the riding hall was one of the few occasions where he could relax, enjoy himself, and outdo some of his classmates.

Rhodes also enjoyed riding and, like Young, chose the cavalry as his branch when he was a senior. In October 1886, anticipating his first day in the riding hall, he wrote: "We begin riding tomorrow, and are glad to get at it. We alternate it with drawing—thus getting more exercise and more time, as the drawing lasts two hours and the riding but one. I have laid in a supply of Vaseline [for chafed inner thighs]. . . . By the time a fellow graduates here he has to be a splendid rider and some of the fancy riders rival circus performers. They—the instructors—generally commence the yearlings with bareback but I guess we'll begin with saddles this year."[18]

The challenge the yearlings faced the first days in the riding hall was more than Rhodes and some of his classmates anticipated. "From this time on until January, we have bareback riding," recalled Rhodes after his first lesson. "Just think of it—and what a circus it is for the people in the gallery, for there is one. In fact 'to see the yearlings ride' every year is one of the sights here. When a lot of green men are put on the slippery backs of not too gentle horses something has to go. It is generally the yearling. . . . John Taylor and Winslow are off half of the time, poor fellows, chasing their horses around the hall."[19]

Guard duty was one of the few occasions when cadets were allowed to miss class or be out of their rooms during mandatory study hours. The academy assigned one senior cadet as the officer of the day to assist a Regular Army officer from the Department of Tactics in patrolling the barracks to report violations of the regulations. During summer camp, in the evenings, and on weekends, cadets stood or marched guard in certain areas of the barracks to assist the officer of the day in enforcing regulations and ensuring safety. It also gave cadets firsthand experience with guard duty, something they would later oversee as officers in the Regular Army.

Rhodes reported this incident while on guard duty: "During my tour the 'long-roll' was beaten, a very unusual occurrence except in case of fire or disturbance. . . . It was only a chimney on fire, which was extinguished without the aid of the Corps. You should have seen the cadets come pouring out of the barracks at the first sound of the drum, and fall in line. . . . We have an engine of which I am brakeman, and one horse-cart. The C Company men form a bucket-brigade and B Company a ladder-corps." Since Young and his friends were members of B Company, he, Harrison, Lamblin, Skerrett, and Webster would have been part of the ladder corps.[20]

Cadets lived in spartan two-man rooms in a four-story barracks with "sinks" (bathrooms) in the cellar. The barracks were modern and comfortable for the time, heated by steam and lit by gas, though the board of directors in 1887 recommended that they be converted to electricity. The barracks were divided into ten "divisions" (hallways), with each division accessed by an iron staircase. Every division had four rooms on a floor, and all the rooms except those in the great towers were the same size.[21] McGlachlin remembered life in the barracks as austere: "The heating of barracks was pretty uneven. Our lighting was with gas and mantles were not furnished for the flames. Water had to be dragged in buckets from hydrants in the area. Bathrooms were distant and not many. All toilet facilities were still further away. A Spartan simplicity in barracks was insisted upon."[22]

The rooms were partitioned into two alcoves on the end farthest from the window, with a crosspiece for curtains. Each alcove contained an iron bedstead against the wall and a row of iron hooks against the partition. Each room was supplied with a stout table, an iron mantel, a double set of open shelves for clothing, a small shelf for helmets and dress hats, a wooden arms rack, and wooden pegs for caps. Each bed had a single mattress, and the two cadets shared a wooden washstand, buckets, and washbowls. Cadets slept on beds with iron crossbars under their mattresses until wire springs were introduced in March 1889.[23]

Every item in the room had its place and order, and the individual cadet was liable to be awarded demerits for the tiniest deviation from regulations. The cadets alternated weekly as "orderly" to sweep and dust everything in the common area of the room outside of the alcoves. From the first of September to the middle of June the cadets could count on a room inspection at least twice a day. They were liable to be "spotted" demerits for a shoe out of place or a speck of dust on the mantel.[24]

When weather permitted, a late-afternoon parade was conducted every day. Parades could be in full dress or a less formal uniform, but arms were always carried. Cadets of the senior class carried sabers, and those of the other three classes shouldered rifles with fixed bayonets. The rifle carried was a Cadet Model 1884 Springfield. Cadets always prayed for inclement weather so they could miss a day's parade. Young surely prayed harder than the rest, since upperclassmen awarded many of his demerits before, during, and after parades.

When dignitaries and foreign guests were present, a parade by the entire Corps of Cadets was a central feature of the visit. Rhodes gave this account of one such visit: "Early part of the week, the Corps was reviewed by Prince Louis Napoleon [of France], and his suite; and the later part, by Prince Kamatsu [of Japan] and his retinue. . . . Gorgeous uniforms . . . broad red stripes on trousers . . . immense swords, thrust through sashes . . . showy blouses and turbans. . . . The Japanese prince needed bracing up. . . . He was all bent over. . . . In showing one of the cadet rooms, the Commandant had one of the smallest Japanese officers stand up alongside of Mr. Mitchell, one of the tallest plebes, nearly six feet, six inches."[25]

Occasionally, a VIP visit would necessitate special parades during hot weather that meant added misery for the cadets. Rhodes registered this complaint in May 1887: "I wish the 'royal blooded' gentry and big men would stay away until June. The last one was a

German prince accompanied by the German minister, Count von somebody. The next, we hear, will be Queen L[iliuokalani] of the Sandwich Islands [Hawaii]. I think the Corps will have a fit if they see General Merritt walking around with the duskey queen."[26]

Two incidents were recorded concerning German visitors' reactions to seeing Young at West Point. According to one account, when a Prussian general was asked what he had liked best about his visit, he replied: "The best thing I saw was a black cadet in charge of a section of artillery." The circumstances of the other description were different, but the answer of the German visitor to the question of what he liked best was: "That black cadet who was a soldier and a gentleman." If true, these incidents indicate that Young was given informal leadership responsibilities as an upper-class cadet and that he performed these well.[27]

Mark Twain's Visit

One VIP the cadets did not mind marching for was Mark Twain. Twain made his third and final known visit during Young's stay at West Point in April 1887, fulfilling a promise made to General Merritt the prior year. Merritt told Twain in an April 17 letter that if he came as scheduled he could observe the artillery drill he missed the previous year. Twain also would have the opportunity to speak to the assembled cadets and officers of the post in the newly refurbished mess hall.[28]

Always eager to visit West Point, Twain must have been delighted to speak to the cadets in the mess hall for another reason. After the mess hall was renovated, it was rededicated and named Grant Hall in honor of the Civil War general and later president Ulysses S. Grant. Twain and Grant had been close friends, and Twain had helped Grant finish his memoir before the general's death in 1885. The dedication of Grant Hall in 1887 was the first time a building at West Point was formally named after someone, and it bears his name to this day.[29]

Twain's wife accompanied him on this visit. On the day before the speech in the mess hall, Merritt treated Twain to a display of artillery drill performed by the cadets. They were joined by Gen. William T. Sherman, his brother Sen. John Sherman, and Dr. Richard Gatling, inventor of the rapid-fire weapon that took his name. According to Rhodes, they fired twenty rounds per gun in the demonstration, competing to see which team could fire the most rounds before the command of "cease firing." Young would have been part of one of the artillery teams, firing cannons as his father did during the Civil War.[30]

Young also would have been present for Twain's performance the following day in the mess hall, a mandatory function for cadets. The *Army and Navy Journal* published this account of the Saturday-evening event in the lavishly decorated mess hall: "[Twain] entered the room with Professor Postlethwaite and was escorted to the platform. The reading this time was on the article that appeared in the April 'Century' 'English as She is Taught'—which aroused simply roars of laughter, but the cream of the fun was in the remark, 'There were donkeys in the Theological Seminary,' and his immediately turning around to explain to the chaplain that nothing personal was intended, was so indescribably funny that the audience continued to laugh and applaud for fully five minutes."[31] The *Journal* went on to say: "On Saturday afternoon the corps of cadets was reviewed by Gen. Merritt. Mr. Clemens was invited to accompany the reviewing party. He committed a court-martial offence by forgetting to throw away his cigar before taking his place in line with the staff."[32]

Twain loved the military pomp and ceremony of West Point, but he never missed an opportunity to tweak the establishment. It was one of his calling cards. Well aware that smoking was forbidden by regulation for cadets, he probably smoked the cigar in the reviewing party for the enjoyment of the corps and the embarrassment of the staff. Between 1881 and 1904, cadets were not allowed to use tobacco in any form.[33] Rhodes commented on this prohibition: "They are awfully down on the use of tobacco here. . . . The penalty is six tours [hours] on the area or twenty 'cons' [hours of confinement], and every few days a fellow is 'hived' [caught]. One 'tac' [tactical officer], known by the soubriquet of 'Slop-Bucket Johnny,' has a habit of coming around at night with a bull's eye lantern, and peering into a fellow's slop-bucket to see if he can find any trace of the use of tobacco."[34]

It is remarkable that despite the threat of severe punishment, cadets were willing to risk smoking. Rhodes reported that there were "many here who smoke incessantly, and are constantly in hot water." He described one particularly gutsy cadet: "I think I saw the 'toughest' thing today since I entered the USMA. One of the first class smoked a cigarette at the dinner table without being caught. . . . That he wasn't seen was short of miraculous!"[35]

Mark Twain would have been pleased.

Second Semester

For Young and his fellow yearlings, the second semester was every bit as difficult as the first. If plebe year witnessed the largest numbers of cadets eliminated by the academic grind, yearling year continued the progression, albeit in smaller numbers. But the second semester of yearling year was the last period when significant numbers of cadets from a year group were found deficient and discharged from the academy. It was an academic breaking point of sorts for Young and his classmates; relatively few would flunk out in their last two years at West Point.

The daily and weekly routine followed by cadets at West Point in this period was rigorous to say the least. General Merritt, in an article written for *The Youth's Companion*, described the routine as follows:

Reveille at 6 A.M. Breakfast 6:30. Recitations [classes] commence at 8 A.M., and continue until 1. Dinner at 1 P.M. Recitations from 2 till 4 P.M. From 4 P.M. till 7 P.M. is devoted to military duties and to recitation.

When the weather permits, a drill of from one hour to an hour and a half is inevitable, and a parade—dress or undress [uniform]—takes place every evening of every day of the year.

At 7 P.M., "call to quarters" is sounded, when every cadet repairs to his room, and, by the regulations, is required to study until 9:30—tattoo—when he may retire for the night.

He must, except when absent on duty, remain in his room from call to quarters in the evening until reveille in the morning, and from 8 o'clock in the morning till 1 o'clock, and again from 2 P.M. till 4 P.M.

Of these hours for study and recitation, each cadet recites from one and one-half hours each morning, to two and one-half hours, and in the afternoon from one to two hours, according to the year's course he is pursuing.

On Saturday the morning is occupied as on other week days; Saturday afternoon is at the cadet's disposal, except that he cannot go beyond the Government lands of the military reservation, and must attend the evening parade.

Sunday is devoted to rest, except that a military inspection under arms, and of the quarters or cadets' rooms in the morning, always takes place. Cadets are required to attend divine service once during Sunday, at either the Roman Catholic or Protestant chapel.[36]

This was Young's daily and weekly routine, without interruption, for the nine months of the academic year. Unlike many of his classmates, he probably never had visitors on weekends or holidays. And he probably was unwelcome at the "hops" or dances that were organized for the enjoyment and distraction of the cadets. Even if he had been allowed to leave the academy grounds, he would have been an unwanted guest in most of the local establishments.

Young's African American predecessor Henry Flipper wrote in his autobiography of this lack of social exchange: "One would be unwilling to believe I had not, from October, 1875, till May, 1876, spoken to a female of any age, and yet it was so. There was no society for me to enjoy—no friends, male or female, for me to visit, or with whom I could have any social intercourse, so absolute was my isolation." Having said this, Flipper moderated his comment about his isolation: "I could and did have a pleasant chat every day, more or less, with 'Bentz the bugler,' the tailor, barber, commissary clerk, the policeman who scrubbed out my room and brought round the mail, the treasurer's clerk, cadets occasionally, and others."[37]

In a letter to his friend John P. Green in Ohio, John Alexander emphasized the general isolation of West Point to the outside world, likening it to being on a secluded peak in the Himalayas. He noted that the isolation was more intense for him, because "most other cadets have friends visiting them and enjoy social advantages at hops and with families of officers which are closed to me." Alexander later commented to a reporter that his experience was not so different from that of his white classmates, saying somewhat sardonically that he "got as much fun out of it as the next man."[38]

For Flipper, Alexander, and Young, life at West Point was not totally devoid of human contact, but they had almost no social interaction with their white classmates. The exceptions to this rule were Skerrett, Bethel, Schermerhorn, Piper, McGlachlin, Webster, Harrison, Lamblin, Haan, Barnum, and Bandholtz. And at least Young could socialize freely with Alexander for his first three years at the academy.

After final exams in June 1887, Young was still in the upper half in French but had fallen in both of his other graded subjects. He dropped to the bottom tenth in math, ranking fiftieth of fifty-three, with three of his classmates failing. He finished dead last in his drawing class, fifty-sixth out of fifty-six. He passed by the skin of his teeth, with an overall order of merit of fiftieth out of fifty-three, with three of his classmates found deficient, all in mathematics. He earned a respectable thirty-one demerits the first semester and nineteen the second.[39]

Uncharacteristically, Rhodes failed to mention in his letters the names of his classmates who were found deficient at the end of the year. Perhaps he was too excited about the upcoming furlough to dwell on negatives, or the three—Samuel Leake, Henry Strickler, and George Woolls—may not have been close enough to Rhodes for him to note their departure.[40]

Graduation

The class of 1887 graduated sixty-four cadets on June 12, 1887. As the members of the graduating class looked forward to their new assignments, the class of 1889 readied their wardrobe for the summer furlough. Young did not share their excitement, since he had already taken his furlough and would stay at West Point for the summer. But at least he could look forward to the graduation speaker, Gen. William Tecumseh Sherman, who had graduated sixth in his class of 1840 and never missed a chance to visit his alma matter.[41]

While the graduates fitted out their new army uniforms, the class of 1889 acquired new clothes for the summer furlough. Most of these cadets had not set foot outside the academy gates since 1885 and had worn nothing but cadet grey for two years. Many had arrived at West Point with only a single set of civilian clothes, which, if still serviceable, was now out of style. They were heading home for ten weeks and wanted a respectable set of clothes to help them look the part of a hometown hero.

One method of making up this clothing deficit was to borrow clothes from other cadets. Preparing for a short summer leave in June 1888, Rhodes wrote his parents: "You need not send any clothes, as I will get enough from my classmates and the plebes to last me. The latter are our great resources, coming as they do directly from 'cit' life with all the latest cuts of clothes which they are glad enough to lend us. I lent mine when I was plebian, and expect to reap the reward of my generosity now." Perhaps Young had assisted Alexander in this fashion two years before, and Alexander returned the favor the previous summer when it was Young's turn to go home on leave.[42]

But many also bought new wardrobes. Armies of tailors arrived in the spring to serve the needs of the graduating class and furloughmen. Rhodes reported before his own furlough that "the tailors were up yesterday—several from New York and Keene from Washington. They transformed the Gymnasium into a show-room and the place was entirely filled with samples. You never saw such a wild crowd of graduates and furloughmen. They were worse than a crowd of fastidious old maids out shopping."[43]

Not every cadet in the class of 1887 was celebrating. At least one, Frederic Evans, was confined to his room and wondering if he would graduate with the rest of his class. Rhodes sympathized with his plight: "Poor Evans was sentenced to be confined to barracks until graduation, and then to camp east of the color line until August 28, the same as I was. Poor fellow, there seems to be one of the graduating class kept back every year. Last year it was Johnson, and the year before Davidson. I am in hopes that the 'Supe' will relent before he leaves and allow him to graduate with his class." Rhodes's comment about one cadet firstie being held back each year would prove prophetic regarding Young.[44]

The superintendent did not relent, but the president of the United States did. President Cleveland signed an executive order on June 16, 1887, remitting the balance of Evans's punishment and "reliev[ing] him from further punishment." Even though the president's order came four days after the rest of his classmates graduated, Evans retained his order of merit, ranking fifty-sixth out of sixty-four. The academy granted him a leave of absence of two months before he reported to his infantry assignment on the western frontier.[45]

Among those to whom General Sherman handed a diploma was Cadet John H. Alexander. In addition to being the second African American to graduate from the U.S. Military Academy, Alexander graduated thirty-second of sixty-four in the class of 1887. He chose cavalry as his branch and was posted to the Ninth U.S. Cavalry, one of the Buffalo Soldier regiments. He and Young would later serve together on the western frontier with this storied regiment.[46]

Thanks to Alexander's graduation, Young had at least one African American visit him at the academy. John Alexander scrimped and saved to have his mother, Fannie Alexander, travel from Arkansas to West Point to share his triumph. Fannie, a former slave, was treated with "the greatest consideration by both the professors and students." The three must have celebrated together Alexander's graduation and commissioning, and the two certainly wished Charles good luck before heading west for John's well-earned graduation leave.[47]

It is not clear what Young and his "five-year" classmates did during the two summer months when the rest of the class of 1889 took their furloughs. They likely stayed at the academy and did some sort of military training, perhaps assisting the leadership cadre run the summer encampment. In 1887 West Point added the practice of "extra instruction," so this is another possibility. This new practice of having professors tutor cadets with academic problems would save Young's career two summers later.[48]

6. Cow Year Alone

Patience and tenacity of purpose are worth more
than twice their weight of cleverness.

THOMAS HENRY HUXLEY

Charles Young's second-class year, which began the summer of
1887, was most likely his loneliest. This was the first year he
was not able to share a tent or barracks room with another African
American cadet. Alexander graduated with the class of 1887, and
no new black cadets entered West Point in June. Young faced his
fourth year at West Point as alone as he had ever been, since no
white cadet would room with him.

Young was given no formal leadership positions that involved
supervision of white cadets during the academic year. But it was
just as well, since he had his hands full with his studies. This was
a doubly difficult year for him, since the third-year curriculum did
not include language or humanities courses to offset his difficulties
in the hard sciences. Still, on the positive side, he seemed to slowly
gain more acceptance and recognition from his classmates with each
succeeding year.

Cow Year

The second-class ("cow") year served as an important break point
for a number of reasons. First, during the summer between the
completion of yearling year and beginning of cow year, cadets normally enjoyed a ten-week furlough, their first break from West Point
in more than two years. The term *cow* came from their celebrated
return from the furlough, when the new senior class lined up on the
Plain to rush and meet the returning second class when the "cows

came home." The superintendent may have succeeded in outlawing the traditional melee in 1886, but the nickname stuck.[1]

Cow year was also the first year that cadets were given any leadership responsibilities of importance. Twenty-two third-year cadet sergeants wore two chevrons on the upper sleeves of their uniforms: one sergeant major, one quartermaster-sergeant, four first sergeants, and sixteen platoon sergeants. The sergeants were charged with the accountability and discipline of their companies and assisted the first-class officers in running day-to-day operations. It reflected badly on them if the cadets in their charge had leadership or academic difficulties. Reminiscent of yearling year, Young's leadership abilities were not tested like those of his classmates.[2]

As in the previous year, Young and the five other surviving turnbacks did not spend the summer with the rest of their classmates. The previous year, Young had spent the ten weeks of summer at home on furlough while his new yearling classmates drilled in the summer encampment. This year the roles reversed, as Young spent most of the summer training on the Plain while McGlachlin, Piper, and the others were on leave.

However, sometime during the summer Young was granted a short summer leave. It was routine for five-year cadets to be granted special summer leaves during their "extra" summer. According to a note that Young's widow, Ada, wrote to Alexander Piper in 1939, he took one or two of these. In this letter, she asked Piper: "Do you remember the name of the classmate living in Philadelphia or somewhere in Pennsylvania with whom Colonel Young spent part of the summer on two occasions?"[3]

Piper responded to Ada's query but could not give a definitive answer. He guessed it might have been Edward Stockham, who lived across the river from Philadelphia in Camden, New Jersey; A. R. Smith, who lived near Philadelphia; or James Jarvis, who came from Pittsburgh. The latter two cadets did not graduate. But the question remained a mystery even after Piper asked the twenty assembled members of the class at their fiftieth reunion. Except for Piper, none of the cadets mentioned in Young's Liberia letter came from Pennsylvania.[4]

Piper was an "army brat" who grew up on East Coast military

posts with his father, Capt. James W. Piper, Fifth U.S. Artillery. The Pipers had deep roots both in Pennsylvania and at West Point. Although Alexander's father was not an academy graduate, his uncle, grandfather, and great-grandfather were all West Pointers. When his father died in 1876, he went to live at West Point with his uncle, Maj. Alexander Piper, class of 1851, who was an artillery instructor. He remained at the academy until his uncle was reassigned in 1881.[5]

Piper then moved to Carlisle in Cumberland County, Pennsylvania, to live with another uncle. He was fifteen when he moved to Pennsylvania, and he attended public schools in Carlisle until he was appointed to the academy in 1885. How he came to be appointed by Cong. Theodore F. Singiser of Idaho Territory is a mystery. Perhaps there were too few qualified candidates in the sparsely populated territory. More likely it had to do with political connections and the fact that Singiser was born and later buried in Cumberland County, not far from Carlisle.[6]

In his letter to Ada, Piper wrote that "Young, like many others in the Class, was never obtrusive, led a quiet life, and paid strict attention to all duties. He was never forcibly brought before the Class in any way because he never did anything that would call particular attention to him. The members of the Class were always friendly with him, and I remember many instances in which he would go to a member of the Class and ask for assistance in his mathematics or some other study, and it was always freely and gladly given."[7]

Furlough

While Young spent the summer drilling on the Plain, Piper and the rest of his classmates enjoyed their ten weeks of freedom from the academy. McGlachlin briefly recounted his experiences on furlough: "We went on furlough and at home I resumed my life that I had been accustomed to there, possibly with a little more importance because I became a sort of leader in dances and gave more attention to girls and had more time to myself than other lads of my age." He also noted that he wore the first white pants—part of his cadet uniform—seen on a man in Stevens Point, Wisconsin. Unfortunately for McGlachlin, after he wore them they came back from the local laundry creased the wrong way and he was unable to wear them again. Perhaps Young had similarly worn the first white pants seen in Ripley the previous summer.[8]

Traditionally, the furlough class arranged to meet for dinner in New York City the night before their return to West Point—their last chance to blow off steam. "We had our furlough dinner in New York, a riotous affair, and saw some comic opera," McGlachlin recalled. "At the end of furlough we met there, most of us, and went up the river on a day-boat, a tumultuous occasion. Everybody seemed a lot older. Hats were broken, ties pulled off, collars distorted, and we presented the conventional appearance for our traditional photograph on the chapel steps."[9]

Rhodes wrote no letters while he was home on furlough in Ohio, but he related his class's return on August 28, 1887: "Got to the Point about 12:00 and immediately repaired to barrack, where we reported to Lieutenant [William B.] Homer, the acting Commandant, and donned our uniforms. After that, Winslow was ordered to march us over to camp, where we could hear the boys cheering for us. . . . As it turned out afterwards the fellows had put in a permit asking to have the usual 'rush' on the Plain, but this was 'cut.'"

Rhodes went on to describe the modified rush: "It was all we could do to keep from breaking ranks and giving them a good cheer, but military order was preserved. . . . Lieutenant Homer shouted, 'Dismiss them, Mr. Winslow!' He did so and the next moment, there was a great yell, the earth shook. We met in the center of the camp, and I suppose all the spectators could see was a cloud of dust, caps in the air, and now and then a seething, struggling, crazy mass of humanity."[10] Young would have been a spectator for this rush, waiting alone for his classmates to return to the encampment on the Plain.

Young and the rest of the corps began the year with a new superintendent: Col. John G. Parke of the Corps of Engineers. Parke graduated second in his West Point class of 1849 and was one of the army's most senior engineers. He had been brevetted to major general and commanded the IX Union Corps during the Civil War. His most notable innovation at West Point during his short tenure was the introduction of telephone service in 1887.[11]

Parke, like his predecessor, used his brevet major general rank for informal and ceremonial purposes. On official correspondence he was listed as Col. John G. Parke, Corps of Engineers, Brevet Major General, U.S.A. This was a throwback to the Old Army, when promotions were slow and brevet and volunteer ranks were awarded only during war. Brevet ranks were awarded for gallantry in combat, and volunteer ranks were awarded for service with temporary volunteer units. Officers returned to their permanent ranks after the war. Generally, if the officer was in a mixed command of officers of more than one branch, as at West Point, he could use his brevet rank to determine seniority. In other situations he reverted back to his Regular Army rank.

Lone African American

So the enormous change for Young beginning in the summer of 1887 was his new status as the lone African American in the corps. During his first three years, from Beast Barracks in 1884 until the graduation of the class of 1887, he had always enjoyed the company of at least one other African American cadet at West Point. The graduation of John Alexander in June 1887 ended that succession. This must have been an exceedingly lonely year for Young.

In addition to the presence of Alexander, Young had benefited from the temporary company of a number of African American cadets who were found deficient in academics after a single semester. The last of these was Henry Wilson Holloway, from South Carolina, who entered West Point in September 1886 and left in January 1887 after being found deficient in mathematics. One other, Eli W. Henderson, was nominated in 1887 but failed to gain entrance.[12]

This closing of West Point to African American cadets was no accident. The end of nominations of blacks to the academy coincided with the end of Reconstruction and the beginning of the enactment of Jim Crow laws that codified segregation and discrimination. After Young, no other African American gained admittance to West Point until after World War I, and no African American graduated from the academy until Benjamin O. Davis Jr. did so in 1936.[13]

Rhodes noted that Young's sheer loneliness compelled him to speak German to some of the "foreign shoe-blacks" employed at the academy. Cadets were not always required to polish their own shoes, and sometimes they employed shoeblacks operating out of the basement of the barracks. Young, like Flipper, was forced to seek human contact with the bugler, tailor, barber, commissary clerk, and anyone else with whom he could strike up a conversation.[14]

Young was unable to take advantage of some of the social functions that provided cadets with a break from the academic and disciplinary routine. Cadets held regular dances ("hops") organized by cadet "hop committees." One of the most important duties of the hop committee was to invite women for those cadets without dates. The success of the hop committee was judged chiefly on the number of women they invited.

Dances and hops became huge social events. The West Point news section of the gossipy *Army and Navy Journal* reported details of these formal affairs, such as the seating assignments of cadets and the single women who attended. Young's classmate Edwin Cole penciled details in his dance card from one such summer of 1888 event, including whom he danced with and what they danced. His list included twenty different women with whom he danced a total of twenty-five times, the dances including waltzes, polkas, and "Germans."[15]

There were important differences among types of dances. A hop was a more relaxed affair, while a "German" was a more formal dance consisting of intricate figures that were improvised and interspersed with waltzes. Cadets wore full dress uniform, while the women wore long formal gowns. But as Rhodes wrote of one such event, there were "girls from everywhere, of all sizes, conditions and colors, — except black."[16]

First Semester

The course requirements of third-year cadets probably gave pause to Young. He had always counted on his strengths in English and foreign languages to balance out his difficulties in mathematics and the hard sciences. During his cow year, Young battled natural and experimental philosophy (physics), chemistry, drawing, practical military engineering, and the tactics of artillery, infantry, and cavalry.[17]

Young was not the only one to have difficulties with the hard sciences. Chemistry also challenged his friends Frank Webster and De-lamere Skerrett. Skerrett, known for his sense of humor and love of practical jokes, occasionally risked demerits to tweak a professor—to the delight of Young and his classmates. For example, Rhodes recalled that "at a lecture upon 'Heat and Light' delivered to the class of 1889 by the Professor of Chemistry, the latter picked up a lighted candle, and noting Skerrett in the front row of students, asked: 'How is it that by blowing upon this candle I can extinguish the flame?' And 'The Kid' replied, without a quiver of an eye-lash: 'Why yes, Professor! It must be the CO_2 in your breath!'"[18]

During the fall semester, in October 1887, Max Repenhagen, who had been the cadet barber since 1874, retired and was replaced by a barber from one of the best barbershops in New York City. Repen-hagen retired to devote time to the manufacture of his patented razor strop, in which academy officers invested. It is unfortunate that this German barber did not put to paper the stories he heard from cadets he served for more than thirteen years. Perhaps he was one of the civilians with whom Young spoke in German.[19]

In November 1887 the academy granted the cadets a temporary respite from studies for Thanksgiving. "Thanksgiving week will long be remembered as the gayest that we have had in many years," reported the *Army and Navy Journal*. The cadets began with a hop on the Wednesday prior to the holiday. The *Journal* quoted Profes-sor Kendrick as saying that "the girls seem to grow prettier every year, and surely their costumes do." On Thanksgiving Day all duty was suspended, and the cadets enjoyed a huge holiday feast in the mess hall.[20]

The upper three classes of cadets were very careful during the first semester to avoid demerits that might make them ineligible for a short Christmas leave. "So far, my next Christmas leave is safe," mentions Rhodes on November 6, "though I know it is but a bubble! Every day, the cadets see their leaves crumbling away, as they get 'skinned' for some little offense." He observes in early December that the cadets are getting "anxious" about their leaves and notes that Edward Stockham has "busted" his Christmas leave. Rhodes must have been busted at some point himself, since he notes that he celebrated Christmas in the barracks and that six men in his class were out on leave for four days.[21]

McGlachlin, on the other hand, was among the lucky half dozen. "My discipline was so good that I went on Christmas leave," he wrote. "A very few succeeded in that in those days. I know that I had $25.00 in all and we were away five days. Several of us stayed at the Sturtevany House on Broadway, about 28th Str[eet]. The money went a long ways then. We did a little drinking in an unsophisticated way. When I looked back upon that experience a year after I did not care to go again."[22]

Young was never among the fortunate few from the class of 1889 who were granted Christmas leave. He had accumulated thirty-one demerits by December of his yearling year, thirty-two by December of his cow year, and thirteen by November of his first-class year. Young celebrated the Christmas of 1887 as he did all five of his years at West Point: at the academy. The difference this year was the absence of another African American with whom he could celebrate the holiday.[23]

After the January 1888 semiannual exams, Young was struggling. He ranked thirty-second of fifty-two in chemistry, forty-first of fifty-one in philosophy (physics) (with one deficient), forty-fifth of fifty-two in tactics, and forty-seventh of fifty-two in drawing. He earned thirty-two demerits the first semester, but this number fell steadily in the semesters remaining until graduation. Young never had to worry again about receiving excessive numbers of demerits, which was perhaps a sign of grudging acceptance by the corps.[24]

Rhodes registered relief that the examinations were over in a January 1888 letter to his parents. He initially wrote that nobody in the class of 1889 was in danger of failing, but two days later he confirmed that "six men were turned out for another examination, their first one not having been satisfactory." These were Edward Stockham, Frederick Sladen, James Normoyle, Joseph Leitch, Antonio Barrios, and Claude Bryan. Normoyle, Leitch, and Barrios had entered West Point in June 1884 and, like Young, had been turned back.[25]

Rhodes updated his parents a week later: "By the way, poor, poor Sladen, one might say one of the idols of our class, was found deficient at the exam and turned back to the 3rd class. I tell you it was cruel, and they might just as well have let him through as not. But Professor Michie told some of us he thought it for Sladen's good to start afresh. . . . Now we have only one more dangerous examination to work off—that in June. . . . They never 'find' a man in 1st class year, unless he utterly gives up studying, and very few do that." Once again, Rhodes did not realize how prophetic his last sentence was in relation to Young.[26]

Five of the six passed the reexamination. Sladen was turned back a year and eventually graduated with the class of 1890. But as was the case with Wesley Merritt, being turned back a year was no lasting liability in the Regular Army. Sladen had a long and distinguished military career and later returned to West Point as superintendent.[27]

The serving commandant, Lt. Col. Henry C. Hasbrouck, left the academy in February 1888. He had served ably since 1882, the entire time Young was at the academy. McGlachlin judged Hasbrouck "an eminently just, fair, and fine man of superior character," and most of the corps shared his opinion. Hasbrouck was a member of the class of May 1861, and twenty-two members of his graduating class of forty-five fought in the Battle of Bull Run in June 1861. He was the originator of the idea of the Battle Monument, the marble column topped with a statue of "Fame" that was dedicated to the members of the Regular Army who lost their lives in the Civil War.[28]

Hasbrouck was replaced by Lt. Col. Hamilton S. Hawkins, the first commandant since the early years of West Point who was not a graduate of the academy, and the last nongraduate to serve in that post. Rhodes's only comment about the new commandant's arrival was that he "had not seen him yet, — only his daughter, uhem, a very pretty girl!" The attractive daughters and nieces of the members of the faculty never lacked suitors.[29]

Horses, Sports, and Social Life

One activity Young continued to find both easy and enjoyable was equestrian training. He had grown up handling horses with his father, similar to another West Point graduate from Ohio who had struggled academically, Ulysses S. Grant. Equestrian lessons for the third-year cadets began in October with basic riding techniques in

SUNDAY MORNING INSPECTION.

30. Class of 1889 (West Point Library Special Collections)

31. Room inspection, 1886, from the July 1887 *Harper's New Monthly Magazine* (Author's collection)

WALKING AN EXTRA.

32. Cadets walking the area, 1887 (West Point Library Special Collections)

33. Cadet formation in 1888 with Charles Young in the rear in first-class full dress uniform (U.S. Army War College)

the large cadet riding hall. Later, the cows were "promoted to sabers and spurs" and the training program became more rigorous.

The only known photo (see illustration 21) of Young before his senior year shows him with his classmates mounted on horseback during cavalry drill. Wearing equestrian uniforms, Young and his classmates posed for the photo on the Plain lined up in a column, four abreast. Since none of the cadets were wearing stripes on their sleeves and they were outside the riding hall, this must have been taken during cow year. Young sat somewhat lower in the saddle than the other cadets in the second file.

Not all cadets were natural horsemen like Young, however, and the riding sessions could be dangerous. Rhodes reported one mishap in a February 1888 letter: "Well we 'won our spurs' last week . . . and a horse little relishes a pair of spurs. Well the upshot of it was that Daddy Winslow's horse got frightened in the riding hall, slipped on the turn, and fell and rolled over Daddy, some say twice. We all thought Dad was killed; even Captain Dorst, our drill-master. He was carried off to the hospital unconscious and did not recover consciousness for several hours. It was found he had suffered a fracture of the thigh—not a bad break, the doctor says."[30]

A few days later, Rhodes reported that Winslow was "getting along fine" and that his classmates were envious of "his comfortable bed in the hospital." The academy built a new cadet hospital in 1884, just south of the mess hall, so the facility must have been state-of-the-art. Winslow ranked number one in his class, and though he would be laid up in bed for two months, Rhodes predicted that missing so many recitations would "not make the slightest difference in his class standing." He was right, as Winslow graduated first in his class in 1889.[31]

McGlachlin also wrote about boating on the Hudson River. He described how he and Ralph "Fat" Harrison amused themselves rowing on the river. They were on their honor while on rowing permit not to go outside certain limits. However, they had a means to get around this restriction: "But we often ran out of camp and, by arrangement with an Engineer sergeant, got a boat. We often went far outside limits and on two or three occasions were able to get together stuff to make some very poor punch."[32]

Rhodes delighted in reporting on West Point's social life and scandals. He recounted a rumor concerning the tactics instructor, Lt. Francis Darr, class of 1880, the same lieutenant who busted Rhodes for mistreating a plebe during summer camp. Rhodes took pleasure in reporting that Darr had run off to South America with another officer's wife. Darr resigned his commission in September 1887, became a successful coffee planter, and was appointed the U.S. vice consul in Guatemala in 1888, a position obtained through the influence of Young's Guatemalan classmate Antonio Barrios.[33]

The tragic figure in this scandal was Lt. John Totten, a well-liked Spanish instructor whose wife ran away with Darr. Rhodes felt sorry for "Sir" John, as he was known among the cadets, and commented, "it must be very hard for Totten to stay here and look a gossiping world in the face." Totten's wife came from a highly respected family who denied the story until it became public knowledge. The whole affair was ugly and played out for months in the newspapers, generating painful publicity for the superintendent and West Point.[34]

Fortunately, scandals at West Point were few and the social life at the academy usually more subdued. The faculty frequently invited cadets to have dinner or tea at their homes, though it is unlikely that Young ever participated in such social events. In September 1887, Rhodes wrote that "six of us went to tea last night at Capt. Metcalfe's." Henry Metcalfe was the head of the Department of Ordinance and Gunnery.[35] The superintendent also entertained cadets. Rhodes boasted: "Had an invitation to take tea at Gen. Parke's. . . . There were five of us cadets invited, with Miss Alden, daughter of the Surgeon, Miss Rogers of W— —, she who used to sit in front of us at the Epiphany, and Miss Parke. Had quite a very pleasant time and we all voted Gen. Parke a brick. He is very informal and fatherly in his manner towards cadets, and related tales of his cadet days here with much gusto."[36]

The day after tea at Captain Metcalfe's, nine members of the class of 1889 played baseball while a few others watched. "We had a great game of baseball yesterday," Rhodes wrote, "between our class and the 'yearlings' in which we came out victorious by a score of 25 to

8. I surprised myself by getting in two home runs, and as a result was presented with a gourd of pure spring water. Ben Johnson bet against us, and Winslow, the winner, had a 'spread' for the nine in the evening off the money won." The yearlings got their revenge, though, beating the cows badly during a rematch the following spring.[37]

The amount of money wagered on the game could not have been large. Cadets earned a meager salary, and they were not allowed to receive money from their families. But there were few things to spend money on and hardly any opportunities for short trips away from the academy. Rhodes complained: "Today I draw my little $90 for the two months. Wouldn't like to work all my life as I am now for $1.50 a day." However, the cadets received full room and board in addition to pay. And Young could boast it was more than his father collected as a private in the Civil War.[38]

Cadets apparently did not mind spending money on sports equipment. In May 1888, Young's classmate Edwin Cole applied for permission to borrow money from his cadet account to purchase a dozen tennis balls for five dollars, with the cost split among Cole, Skerrett, Lassiter, and Francis Lacy. 1st Lt. Jacob Galbraith disapproved the request, opining: "The game itself is strongly approved—But the applicant being in debt it would be better to obtain cheaper balls." There are a number of other contemporary accounts of cadets playing tennis.[39]

March 1888 witnessed a terrible blizzard that piled snow fifteen feet high in places and left the academy isolated from the outside world for more than a week. No supplies could get through, and rations were cut in half. The cadets amused themselves with snowball fights and by jumping out of upper-story barracks windows into snowdrifts. Out of necessity, the commandant allowed cadets to walk back to the barracks individually from their meals, picking their way through snowdrifts, rather than marching in formation. This break from routine, as always, delighted the cadets.[40]

Henry Irving

The snowstorm could not prevent the West Point performance of Henry Irving, the greatest English actor of his time. A friend of

Prof. Peter Michie's, Irving arranged to bring his acting company to the academy free of charge. According to McGlachlin, Irving closed his theater in New York and was transported to West Point at no expense by the West Shore Railroad. The performance took place on March 19, 1888, and, like the Twain recitals, was open to cadets, officers, and their families. Young surely attended the performance.[41]

Irving was one of the most influential and famous actors to ever reach the English stage. At the height of his career when he visited West Point in 1887, Irving took his company on eight tours across North America between 1883 and 1904. In 1895 he became the first actor in British history to be knighted. When the Dramatic and Literary Society of London gave him a welcome-home dinner in London in June 1900 after he returned from the United States, Mark Twain was on hand to propose a toast to Sir Henry Irving.[42]

McGlachlin gave a glowing report of the program: "A temporary platform of boards was erected in Grant (the Mess Hall) and the scenery was so simple and the pieces of furniture so few that not much change would be made on the stage. So over the proscenium arch were hung improvised signs to tell us what were the scenes. From [the] barracks we saw Miss [Ellen] Terry walking and of course we all fell in love with her. The play was wonderful. . . . That show thrills me still."[43] Rhodes added: "Henry Irving and Miss Terry gave us a splendid performance of the 'Merchant of Venice.' It took place in the Mess Hall on an improvised stage but the latter only seemed to make the actors more eager to excel. Critics of whom there were a number representing all the leading N.Y. papers, say the company never did better. . . . They surely never had a more enthusiastic audience. . . . Miss Terry as Portia was superb, and Irving played the Jew to perfection."[44]

Once the performance ended, the cadets rose to their feet and applauded until Irving returned to the stage and gave a speech. After joking with the cadets, he concluded: "Tonight it may be, the joy-bells are ringing far off in London, —for (here we all wondered what was coming) it is the first time that a British Army has captured West Point!" This last statement alluded to the unsuccessful attempt by the famous Revolutionary War traitor, Benedict Arnold, to sell the plans of West Point to the British army.[45]

In the same letter containing details of the Irving visit, Rhodes mourned the loss of another classmate. James Lamblin of Georgia resigned in order to take the place of his father as a professor at a college when the latter died unexpectedly. Lamblin was another member of the small circle of friends Young mentioned in his Liberia letter. McGlachlin, Lamblin's roommate, had this to say about his departure: "The army lost the making of a fine officer, I lost a good friend and constructive influence on my life. I never saw him again, for it was not long until he died."[46]

Second Semester

The second half of his cow year, Young continued to feel the pressure of academics. He finished forty-first of forty-nine, with one of his classmates found deficient, in chemical physics, mineralogy, and geology; forty-fourth of forty-seven, with three deficient, in philosophy (wave motion and astronomy); and dead last once again in drawing. He completed the year ranked forty-sixth of forty-seven in general order of merit, with three of his classmates found deficient. As in his previous year, Young was dangerously near the point of being declared deficient.[47]

What may have saved Young during the first or second semester of his cow year was a rapport he developed with 1st Lt. William Gordon. Gordon was an ordnance officer and assistant professor under Professor Michie in the Department of Natural and Experimental Philosophy, known today as physics. The cadets referred to this subject as "phil," and "phil" and "chem" were the most dreaded courses of cow year. Gordon was one of two professors mentioned in Young's Liberia letter who had shown him "disinterested help."

Young struggled during his cow year chiefly with physics, and this subject, combined with chemistry and drawing, caused his academic ranking to plummet precipitously. Precisely what help Gordon provided to Young is unknown. Since Young had difficulty with "phil" in both semesters, it is possible that Gordon undertook some sort of tutoring with him. Tutoring may have saved Young and other cadets under pressure of failing physics in the first semester and wave motion in the second semester.

McGlachlin mentioned another of Young's classmates who benefited from such tutoring. John Martin was a member of the class of 1889 who, like Young, came from Ohio. The problem with Martin, according to McGlachlin, was that he was "badly prepared" academically: "He was naturally military and a tireless and conscientious worker. He would probably have been found had not one of the instructors undertaken to coach him privately. Once well started he did very well, graduating high."[48]

It is possible that Professor Gordon helped Young in another way. Years later a friend of Young's related the following story: "It must not be thought, however, that Young was without friends in the institution. When one of his instructors came to realize the effects of forced solitude upon him, this official advised Young to put in a requisition for a horse which he would see that he got." This allowed Young to get away from the barracks and take rides in the countryside surrounding the academy. Perhaps Gordon helped mitigate Young's loneliness in this way.[49]

The other subject Young had great difficulty with was drawing, which was an essential skill for an officer, even if he was not a member of the Corps of Engineers. Army officers were required to sketch enemy positions and map unknown terrain while performing reconnaissance missions. Some of Young's original sketches from his West Point portfolio are reproduced in this book (see illustrations 22–27). If Young finished last in his class in drawing, then some of his classmates must have been as talented as James Whistler, who had attended West Point thirty years earlier.[50]

Young's poor grades in drawing did not come from lack of effort. During Young's first semester as a yearling, officials awarded him demerits for drawing-related offenses on three occasions. In one incident the instructor gave him demerits for "taking a disapproved drawing from Drawing Academy without . . . permission," and on another for "neglecting instructions in drawing [a] colored map" (perhaps illustration 22 in this book). On the last occasion, an officer reported Young for "drawing and sketching in [the] window of [the] guard house."[51]

Thirty-two sketches in Young's drawing portfolio from his year-ling or cow year have survived. Most are black-and-white drawings done in pencil or charcoal, and only eight are in color, the latter depicting mainly buildings or terrain features. Years later, as a military attaché, Young used his drawing skills to sketch maps of much of the inland and coastal features of Haiti, maps that were employed when the U.S. Navy and Marines invaded the island in 1915.[52]

John Alexander probably did one of the color paintings in Young's portfolio. How it came to be in Young's possession is a mystery, but perhaps it was a gift. The back of the painting of a woman was covered with scribbles. And aside from the fact that "John H. Alexander" was signed several times in the doodling, a handwriting analysis showed it was Alexander's. This may point to a closer relationship between Young and Alexander.[53]

In April 1887, Rhodes, who had no difficulty in drawing, reported on news from a former member of the class of 1889, James Schermerhorn. Though Schermerhorn had resigned plebe year, he kept in touch with Young and the rest of his classmates for many years. Schermerhorn by this time was a successful journalist, and Rhodes noted that he had received the State of Michigan first prize in 1888 for an essay entitled "Hazing at West Point." During a surprise visit to West Point the following year, Schermerhorn received permission to accompany his former classmates to the barracks and the mess hall. He probably spent some time with Young on this visit.[54]

Final exams spanned the first week of June 1888. Rhodes reported soon afterward that the academy administered a second exam to Stockham, Normoyle, Barrios, Bryan, Bethel, Burkhardt, and Winston because of poor results on their first. Young was noticeably absent from the list. Rhodes thought at the time that most of them had made it through, but three days later he informed his parents that two of the six had been found deficient. Claude Bryan was found in "chem" and "phil," while Eddie Winston was deficient in "phil."[55] Bryan was finished as a cadet and caught the first transportation home. He later became the commandant of a military school at Niagara, New York, and taught mathematics, French, and tactics. Winston, who had entered with Young in 1884 and had been turned back once already, was no quitter. Rhodes reported later in June that

Winston had been to the War Department and convinced someone to get him reinstated. Rhodes announced Winston's triumphant return to West Point in July. Winston evidently learned his lesson, because he was never again in academic trouble and graduated with the class of 1889.[56]

Graduation took place on June 12, 1888. The class of 1888 graduated only forty-four, one of the smallest classes in years. As the new second lieutenants of the class of 1888 journeyed to their new assignments, the class of 1889 took over as the new first class. Clement Flagler became the first captain, and George Langhorne, William Lassiter, and John Martin were made the other cadet captains, each commanding one of the four companies of cadets. Rhodes was content to be promoted to cadet lieutenant. Young faced another year as a cadet private.[57]

Young had thus far successfully completed the curriculum required for graduation from West Point, but he had a difficult year ahead. Having finished next to last in his class during cow year, he had precious little room to maneuver if he wanted to avoid becoming the immortal of the class of 1889. Young's first-class year would prove his most challenging, but at least he could take comfort in its being his last.

7. Firstie Year and Graduation

> West Point has given birth to but one traitor in all of its glorious history and Benedict Arnold was not a black man.
>
> CHARLES YOUNG

Charles Young probably had mixed feelings about his senior year, which began in the summer of 1888. He faced his last year at West Point as the only African American at the academy. Although he had begun to win the grudging acceptance of some of his classmates, many continued to treat him like a pariah. The only bright spots for Young were the small circle of eight classmates who showed him friendship, an increasing number of classmates who recognized his strength of character, and a few instructors who sympathized with his plight.

Young served in no formal leadership positions his senior year, as had been the case in his previous two years as well. Still, he had earned his senior standing and could wear proudly the feathered plume and cadet saber that marked the uniform of a first classman. Most importantly, he could take consolation in this being his last year at the academy and could look forward to his commissioning and first assignment in the U.S. Army as a second lieutenant.

Firstie

A cadet's first-class ("firstie") year was the high point of his West Point career. He had survived the previous three years of academics and successfully run the disciplinary gauntlet fashioned to trip him up at every turn. The reward for those who had excelled was a position of command and responsibility in the corps, but Young did not rank high enough among his classmates to be considered for such a position.

Even those who did not wear stripes were accorded the prestige and privileges associated with being a first classman. Stripes or no stripes, all firsties carried sabers rather than shouldering heavy rifles during drill and parade. They also wore tall, drooping, black cocks' feather plumes on their dress parade helmets instead of the black worsted pom-poms worn by the rest of the classes.[1]

There are only three known photographs of Young as a cadet, and two of these were taken during his firstie year. Official photos of cadets were not taken in those days, but Pach Brothers of New York City sent a professional photographer to West Point once a year to take pictures of those who desired. The photographer took individual photos of those cadets who chose to pose and also took a group photo of each class present at the academy. Additionally, the War Department periodically sent Signal Corps photographers to West Point to document and publicize the academy.

A photographer from the Signal Corps took the first picture of Young as a firstie during the 1888 summer camp, wearing full dress gray, a saber, white cross belt, white gloves, and a black 1869 model dress hat with plume (see illustration 33). Young stands at attention in the rear of summer camp formation, his posture straight but less rigid than that of the plebes in the ranks in front of him. Unlike the cadet lieutenant first classman inspecting the rifle of one of the plebes in the front rank, he was wearing no stripes on his sleeves. All of the other cadets in the formation appear to be plebes, with the exception of a single yearling corporal at the end of the first rank. The photographer caught a cadet frozen forever peeking out of the tent flap behind Young.

The second photo of Young is an individual photograph taken of him in 1889 by the Pach photographer (see illustration 15). It is a solemn and unsmiling study of Young, who was clad in full dress uniform, long gray overcoat open at the collar, and dark kepi hat perched on his head. His eyes, fixed on the camera, demand respect. Young's overcoat is unbuttoned, and the pose is uncharacteristically informal for such a picture. A survey of his classmates' posture reveals that most chose a more formal half profile. Perhaps Young chose the pose for a reason.

Cadets could purchase an album from Pach Brothers in Russian or Moroccan leather with their choice of individual, group, and West Point views. The 1889 order form listed seventy-nine individual "officers," from President Harrison down the chain of command to Master of the Sword Koehler. All forty-nine members of the class of 1889 were listed, along with seven former members of the class, twenty-six different groupings, and eighty-three other academy views. The albums sold for the princely sum of twenty dollars for the large and twelve for the small, not including the price of the individual photos, which ranged from twenty-five cents to one dollar. [2]

It was significant that Young was never present in any of the class of 1889 group photos taken during his years at West Point. The academy published official annuals in later years, but Stoddard Publishers was the only one to offer an official-looking pictorial beginning in 1887. These included photos of each class grouping and depictions of the academic buildings and the cadets in training. They used Pach Brothers images, and Young was conspicuously absent from the group photos of the class of 1889 for the years 1887, 1888, and 1889. Although a small number of cadets were missing from the class picture each of the three years, no cadet other than Young was missing in all three years. Either he was not invited or he chose not to participate—perhaps both. [3]

Stripes and Pranks

The first class ran the day-to-day operations of the Corps of Cadets, which was organized into a battalion of four companies. The most prestigious positions for the new seniors were the four cadet captaincies. Clement Flagler was the first among equals, or first captain, and commanded A Company. Young's friend George Langhorne commanded B Company, to which Young belonged. The other two captains were William Lassiter, commanding C Company, and John Martin, commanding D Company. All four wore the badge of their rank, four oversized stripes on their upper arms that struck absolute fear in the hearts of plebes and awe in the eyes of all others. [4]

There were also a number of positions for cadet lieutenants, who wore three stripes on their upper arms. These included an adjutant, a quartermaster, and twelve platoon leaders, one for each of the three platoons in every company. Charles Rhodes, Alexander Piper, and Walter Bethel were among the lieutenants who commanded the platoons. But the majority of the firsties were cadet privates, since there were forty-nine surviving members of the class of 1889 and only eighteen positions for officers. Young and McGlachlin were modest members of this group of firstie privates who had few if any leadership responsibilities.[5]

But as Rhodes had found out as a yearling, stripes were as easy to lose as they were to earn. The first casualty Rhodes reported was Cadet Lt. Alvin Sydenham. "Sydenham was 'busted' yesterday," he wrote on September 22, 1888, "for allowing some members of the riding platoon to lag behind and get some apples the other day, while we were taking a ride on the road." The chain of command replaced him as a lieutenant with Albert D'Armit.[6] Another lieutenant lost his hard-earned stripes not long after Sydenham. According to Rhodes, "Poor Jackie Hains has lost his chevrons, trying to answer embarrassing questions, fired at him by a very nice Miss Biddle, which indicated to Lieutenant [John] Biddle, —who was present, that Jack was taking dinner at the Biddle's hospitable board, without authority. . . . Miss Biddle feels dreadfully over it. . . . Biddle, who is the salt of the earth, was torn between his duty to report all delinquencies, and his duty as host to his sister's dinner-guest. He had to follow his conscience!"[7]

Some cadets got away with practical jokes that should have earned them a reduction to the ranks. A cadet could earn a great deal of notoriety if he carried out a spectacular or daring prank, especially if he could do so without getting caught. It was a paradox in this environment of iron discipline and rigid regulations that such risk taking was admired by cadets and winked at by the faculty. Perhaps it was just a matter of tolerating harmless fun and letting off steam. But another explanation might be that the daring, courage, and success of such acts were esteemed for their value and application in warfare.

Rhodes detailed one example: "[A] cannon was fired out on the plain by some of the boys causing some excitement on the post. When I got back to the barracks I heard that the cadets had attached a string to a cannon-ball and stretched the string across a path, so that some soldiers, returning from stables, came by it, disengaged the cannonball, pulled the lanyard, and fired the gun! The cadets meanwhile, being safely ensconced in their rooms."[8] It would not be a stretch to say that this type of audacity, planning, and execution might be good training for the battlefield. It certainly provided fodder for stories swapped among cadets, which only grew in daring and scale in the retelling years after graduation. Cadets still marvel at the story of Cadet Hugh Johnson, class of 1903, who disassembled the reveille cannon and reassembled it on top of the clock tower.[9]

Cadet captains also ran the risk of losing their chevrons, and sometimes they did so on purpose. Rhodes related the story of how their first captain lost his stripes: "Flagler our first captain, made an intentional breach of confinement yesterday, and so will probably be relegated to the ranks. . . . He has had some provocation for this getting out of the Captaincy, as he had not been treated very well this year by the 'tacs.' So he got mad, and as we are not allowed to resign our cadet commissions, he took this way—a foolish way I think—of getting into ranks."[10] Flagler got his wish and was busted to cadet private in November 1888. He apparently did not get along with the officer from the Department of Tactics assigned to his company. George Langhorne moved up to first captain, and Charles B. Hagadorn filled the vacant captain slot in the battalion of cadets. Cadet Privates McGlachlin and Young must have viewed the whole affair with bemusement.

This game of musical first captains seemed destined to continue. Langhorne almost lost his stripes before they were sewn on. As Rhodes recounted in early December, "Langhorne made a breach of confinement yesterday—it was an intentional one, so that he will probably be reduced, a' la Flagler." Rhodes explained: "George was in confinement all day. During the afternoon he waited until he was inspected, and then went out calling on the post, intending to return before the next inspection. But he did not do so and the officer of the guard inspected while he was absent." Rhodes penned a note later that evening that "Langhorne got out of his scrape on a technicality much to the surprise of the whole Corps," and he retained his first captain position through to graduation.[11]

George Tayloe Langhorne was another of those whom Young mentioned in his Liberia letter as having shown him kindness and friendship while he was a cadet. Langhorne, like Young, was born in Kentucky, but he was raised in Virginia as part of an old, well-established family. Langhorne proved a natural leader and, as Young discovered later, was a good man to have as a friend at West Point.[12]

First Semester and Branch

Young continued to struggle academically the first semester of his firstie year, even though he again had some liberal arts courses to buoy his overall ranking. He finished the semester in January 1889 at thirty-third of forty-nine in law, thirty-fourth of forty-nine in history, forty-first of forty-seven in ordnance and gunnery (with two cadets deficient), and forty-eighth of forty-nine in civil engineering. Despite his low class ranking, he must have breathed a sigh of relief at having successfully completed his second-to-last semester.[13]

The two cadets found deficient in ordnance and gunnery—Hagadorn and Langhorne—were not cashiered and sent home, however. According to Rhodes, the academy "conditioned" the two in ordnance until May, when they were given another examination. Both passed this exam and had their conditional status revoked. Perhaps what Rhodes said at the end of cow year was correct, that the academy "never find[s] a man his first class year, unless he utterly gives up studying."[14]

The higher a cadet graduated in his class (calculated in terms of class ranking in academics and leadership), the better his chances for choice branch assignments in the Regular Army. The top five or six graduates in the class almost always secured coveted assignments in the Corps of Engineers. The next ten cadets mainly chose artillery, the next most prestigious branch. The dash and glamour of the cavalry branch appealed to the middle of the class, while infantry brought up the rear. Exact numbers of branch assignments available to the graduating class were based on the army's actual needs.

In the Old Army, cadets could pick only a branch and regimental assignment in a unit that had an actual vacancy for a new second lieutenant. Essentially, an officer had to get promoted, retire, or die in a regiment to create a vacancy. This caused problems for the army and the academy when too few vacancies existed in the field to cover the assignments of all the cadets graduating in a particular year. Fortunately for the class of 1889, in May 1886 Congress passed a law that allowed cadets to join regiments as "supernumerary" (additional) second lieutenants until an actual position opened. This would have important implications for Young later.[15]

The only other route to a commission as a second lieutenant was from the ranks. Noncommissioned officers or sergeants who showed promise and passed an officer's examination could be commissioned as officers (Young would successfully tutor Benjamin O. Davis Sr. for this exam in 1901), but this occurred fairly infrequently, and academy graduates generally looked down upon these "rankers." Rhodes chafed at the idea that it had "become easier to gain a commission by enlisting than by passing through the Point." The possibility worried Rhodes in January 1889, when he remarked: "Our class is also much exercised over the confirmation the coming week by the Senate of the appointments of eleven noncommissioned officers. This will swallow up eleven Army vacancies and between now and June we cannot hope for more than 20 or 25 vacancies, the remainder of our class will have to take additional lieutenancies. . . . We are pulling wires in the Senate but with little chance of success as General Schofield's son's name goes out at the same time."[16]

The class's efforts to influence the Senate failed. Richmond McAllister Schofield was commissioned a second lieutenant in the Fourth Cavalry on February 11, 1889, just a few weeks after Rhodes wrote his parents. This meant that at graduation there were probably eleven fewer positions available for the cadets in the Regular Army. In an army with an authorized total strength in 1889 of 28,417, of which 2,148 were commissioned officers and 459 second lieutenants, every vacancy mattered.[17]

Officers assigned to the West Point faculty tried to promote their own regiments as the best in terms of assignments or advancement to the graduating cadets. Each infantry, cavalry, or artillery officer posted to West Point was carried on the books of his regiment, and he returned to his units upon completion of his academy assignment. Until an officer attained the field-grade rank of major, he generally served his entire career with his regiment. The only exception was when an officer was detached for special assignments such as duty as a military attaché or teaching at West Point. It was natural for the officers on the faculty to try to recruit for their own regiments those cadets who showed the most promise.

Edward McGlachlin recounted how Professor Peter Michie talked him into choosing artillery. He arrived one evening at the professor's quarters escorting Michie's daughter, Marie: "We arrived at the back gate pretty close to 'call to quarters.' Her father was sitting on the porch and addressed me without the 'Mr.' for the first time. That day or the day before I had written down my preference for [a] commission in the Cavalry. He asked me what had been my choice and I told him. He thought I had made a mistake and advised me to go and change my choice." McGlachlin continued: "I wriggled, of course. I had my cavalry equipment or part of it in my room and had spent considerable time admiring myself with the long orange plume on my helmet. My reply to him, however, was that I would not graduate high enough for the Artillery. He said that it was possible that he knew more than I did about that. I was getting nervous about call to quarters but he held me there telling me the advantages of the Artillery. The next day I went down and chose artillery first, cavalry second." McGlachlin became an artillery officer and never regretted the choice. [18]

Rhodes provided these quixotic reasons for why he was considering cavalry: "Just now, I have the cavalry fever again. . . . It is hard to decide. . . . Cavalry is to my taste. . . . Yet people say that Infantry is the better for promotion. . . . We had such a fine ride, yesterday morning, up over Cro' Nest. . . . Magnificent view from the top looking down the Hudson. I never come home from a ride that I do not come back a cavalryman, in mind and body. . . . Lieutenant [Charles] Braden says he would enlist in a regiment of monkeys, if he could get a promotion." Promotion was clearly uppermost in the minds of both Rhodes and McGlachlin, though the dash of cavalry still held an attraction. [19]

Young's options were more limited, however, since there were only four black regiments, two infantry and two cavalry. The army's policy at this time was to assign African American officers to one of the four black regiments. The two black academy graduates before Young had both gone to one of the Buffalo Soldier cavalry regiments, the Ninth and Tenth U.S. Cavalry. Young's love of horses naturally drew him to the cavalry, but in the end his academic and disciplinary rankings left him few assignment choices. The War Department would also have a final say.

Presidential Election and Bodyguard

It was conventional wisdom that the U.S. military stayed out of politics. But the cadets were very interested and partisan about the presidential election in November 1888, though most of the cadets were too young to vote. Rhodes rejoiced at the Republican victory but noted that a majority of the corps favored the Democrats. Young would have favored the Republicans also, since it was the party of Abraham Lincoln and had been supported by African Americans since the Civil War. Additionally, a Republican congressman had appointed Young to West Point, and Young's father was active in the Republican Party.

The incumbent Democratic candidate, Grover Cleveland, who had saved the firsties from expulsion after the rush of 1887, ran against the Republican nominee, Benjamin Harrison of Indiana. Cleveland had been the first Democratic president elected in the postwar period. Tariff and agricultural reform were the major issues, and Harrison won the election easily.

Rhodes reported after the election: "Isn't the victory glorious with President, Senate, and House Republican. . . . We had a Corps vote on Tuesday and found it Democratic by about [a] 40 majority. [Ben] Johnson, in anticipation of Democratic victory, sent for a dozen red bandannas. We made private arrangements to receive returns all night from the telegraph office. In the middle of the night, the 'tac' surprised an excited crowd of politicians, waiting for the 'courier' and the result was a grand scattering, and two or three reported."[20]

Many of the cadets had their hearts set on participating in the presidential inauguration in Washington DC, scheduled for March

4, 1889. Not willing to stand idly by and let an opportunity pass, they began writing the War Department and their congressmen to lobby for an appearance by the Corps of Cadets. Rhodes mentioned in a letter that Sen. John H. Reagan from Texas, who had a son at West Point, had promised to talk to President Cleveland about extending an invitation to the corps.[21]

The superintendent considered this an example of cadets using political connections to circumvent the leadership at the academy. In late February, Rhodes complained: "The Corps is greatly disappointed that we will not be allowed to attend the inauguration. . . . For our efforts, an order was published last week, forbidding cadets to communicate with the War Department. . . . But it is now 'Water over the Dam.'"[22] The following month, Rhodes consoled himself with the fact that it had rained in Washington during the inauguration and hinted that the corps might travel to New York City the following month as a consolation.[23]

New York City celebrated the centennial of the adoption of the Constitution of the United States with a huge parade on April 30, 1889. The Corps of Cadets was invited to march in the military parade and to act as the president's honorary bodyguard. The entire corps was excited about the event, even though it necessitated battalion drill for an entire week. They were happy to march the extra miles in exchange for an opportunity to see New York City and be excused from classes the following day.[24]

At 5 a.m. on April 30, the entire corps, at that time numbering approximately 250 cadets, along with the West Point band and the West Point officer staff, embarked on the steamer *Mary Powell* and landed at the Battery in New York City after a chilly passage down the Hudson River. After marching up Broadway to Wall Street, they waited for an hour and a half for the procession to begin. They had the honor of being the first unit in the marching column, leading the parade on its entire ten-mile route through the city.

At the halfway point of the march, the corps wheeled into line and waited for the reviewing party. They presented arms when the official party in their carriages approached. Behind the president's carriage rode General Sherman, who had served as the commander of the army from 1869 to 1883 and was now retired. Rhodes recalled of Sherman that "I never saw a man's face so light up as when he turned his face and saw the Corps standing motionless at a 'present.' I guess he thinks more of the Corps of Cadets than most anything on Earth. . . . He always said so."

The cadets ended their march on Fifty-ninth Street and then walked a mile back to the waterfront to board the steamer home. When they arrived at the academy, some of the cadets still had the energy to play baseball, according to Rhodes. Rhodes also mentioned that it was a matter of corps pride that the sick report for the following day be as short as possible, in spite of the long miles marched and hours waiting on their feet. The list was unusually short, and the commandant was "tickled to death."[25]

What Young thought of the parade in New York City is unknown. He was present for the parade, since it was a command performance. As the only African American in the corps at that time, he must have been the object of many comments and stares by the white and black residents of New York City who lined the streets to watch the parade. Young marched in the parade as a cadet private first classman with less than two months to graduation. That alone must have caused him to step out smartly.

Fisticuffs

During Young's time at West Point, cadets occasionally settled arguments or insults with fistfights. Normally, the individuals, their seconds, and any interested cadet spectators went off into the woods surrounding the campus and settled the affair away from the prying eyes and demerit books of the tactical officers. The fights were bare-knuckled and lasted until one of the cadets conceded or was knocked out.

In January 1889, Rhodes reported on two fights. The first involved two members of the plebe class and resulted in one breaking a bone in his hand. The other was between two firsties: Young's friend George Langhorne and a classmate named Morris Barroll from Maryland. It stemmed from an altercation in the mess hall, where Cadet First Captain Langhorne challenged Cadet Private Barroll's insubordination. It was customary for Langhorne to handle this privately rather than report the matter to the authorities.[26]

Surprisingly, Young was the cause of the fight. According to a report in the *Cleveland Gazette*, the incident stemmed from Young's seating assignment. Langhorne had assigned Young to a "staff table," but because of complaints from his messmates he was reassigned to a different table. At Young's new table, Barroll took insult and protested so loudly and rudely that Langhorne felt compelled to confront him. [27]

The *New York Herald* reported that the "Duel in the Ring" resulted in sixteen bloody rounds and four black eyes. Rhodes failed to report the winner but gave this description of the aftermath: "I saw the accounts of the Barroll-Langhorne encounter in the *World*, *Herald*, *Philadelphia Press*, *Army and Navy Journal*, etc. It's too bad, I think, that the reporters made so much of it and brought the question of the 'color line' so frequently. It is very strange if *some* fights do not occur among a crowd of two or three hundred young fellows, and might have occurred over the seating of any person in the mess hall as well as Young. I can assure you, there are some white cadets who are a great deal more objectionable as table companions than Mr. Young." One can only wonder what it was, besides the color of his skin, that made Young objectionable to Rhodes. [28]

Another account of a fight involving Young appeared in a lengthy *Washington Post* article a few years after his death. The piece is accurate about Young in most respects, so there is probably some truth in the story, though details and sources are lacking. The article notes that one method Young used to get back at classmates who purposely offended him was to compose a ballad and set it to music to carry the message home. Perhaps he used the irony and double meaning passed down by his parents from African American spirituals. He likely composed his creations in the Dialectic Hall, and perhaps McGlachlin was on hand to hear them. [29]

On one occasion, according to the article, Young's intended victim, "a cadet from the North," took offense at the ballad and challenged "the chastity of the negro's maternal forbearers." This caused one of Young's other classmates, a South Carolinian "who had learned to admire the suavity of the black cadet," to challenge the northerner in Young's stead. Of course, the southerner pummeled the northerner and extracted an apology. According to the story, the incident "broke the ice of silence which had congealed for months about the negro's presence at the Academy." If the incident did take place, it probably occurred during plebe year. Life would have been much easier for Young if reality was as simple as was depicted in the article.[30]

Second Semester

The second semester of Young's firstie year proved every bit as difficult as the first. Law was no problem for him, but ordnance and gunnery was as demanding as it had been the first semester. He had struggled the most with civil engineering the previous fall, and he continued to have trouble with military engineering in the spring semester. 1st Lt. George Goethals, whom Rhodes referred to as a "mean cuss," taught military engineering. The only subject Young had a relatively easy time with was Spanish.

In contrast, Young's friend Delamere Skerrett, nicknamed "The Kid" by his classmates, had a particularly difficult time with Spanish. Rhodes wrote this account of Skerrett to illustrate both his classmate's sense of humor and his difficulty with foreign languages: "When, upon one unhappy occasion, the instructor, 'Sir' John Totten, gave Del[amere] a long English sentence to convert to Spanish, Skerrett gave deep thought to the problem at the blackboard, hoping, as cadets will to 'bugle it.' Finally, the time being short and to hide his evident ignorance, he deliberately erased the last letter of each English word, and replaced them in succession by the vowels 'a,' 'e,' 'i,' 'o,' and 'u.'" According to Rhodes, "Lieutenant Totten glanced at the disguised sentence and remarked: 'Mr. Skerrett, that is the most remarkably Anglicized sentence I've ever seen. You may forthwith bid farewell to your friends in this section!' And then to the amazement as well as delight of the Spanish section, 'The Kid' took Totten at his word, and solemnly made the rounds of the room, shaking hands and saying good-bye to each classmate. Totten himself shook with laughter, and strange to say, never reported 'The Kid' for his audacious prank."[31]

Young continued to earn demerits through his last semester, and some of his infractions are perhaps illustrative of his academic struggles and attempts to cope with his situation. Twice in March 1889 an instructor awarded him demerits for "Book open in hall of Academic Building," which likely indicates that Young must have been attempting some last-minute preparation before class. Cadets were expected to arrive ready for class and were not allowed to open their books or study in the hallways of the academic buildings. Because many had once been cadets themselves, West Point instructors were not shy about handing out demerits to cadets for the tiniest infraction.[32]

One reason Young may not have studied enough before class was music, which remained central to his existence. In March he was given three demerits for "singing in hall of barracks during evening call to quarters," and in May he received seven demerits for "playing piano in Dialectic Hall after call to quarters." Perhaps he was singing or playing the piano when he should have been studying. The previous September he was awarded one demerit for "Guitar not in proper place at AM inspection of tactical officer," so he spent time playing the guitar as well. An official docked Young the last demerit of his cadet career on June 7 when he reported late for reveille.[33]

After final exams in June 1889, Young ranked seventeenth of forty-nine in Spanish, forty-first of forty-nine in law, and forty-seventh of forty-nine in ordnance and gunnery. He was the only one in his military engineering class to be declared deficient by Lieutenant Goethals, although Young and several others had to pass a reexamination in ordnance.[34]

By this time, Young's motivation and determination had won the grudging admiration of most of his classmates and professors. According to Rhodes in an obituary written for the Association of Graduates in 1923, Young had gained ground each of his years at West Point, and by his fifth year "his own class began to acknowledge and respect his finer traits of character; while a spirit of fair play induced many cadets of character and standing in the Corps to treat Young with the kindness and consideration which had long been his due."[35]

But what Rhodes said in a letter to his parents in June 1889 offered a different slant: "Mr. Young did very poorly in both Engineering and Ordnance and was given a special written examination in each branch afterwards. Taylor, Kemp and Webster were also examined subsequently in Ordnance, but I think they all pulled through O.K. I hope the darkey got through. It would be a terrible disappointment to him after five years of work to lose the coveted diploma just as he was about to grasp it. Although I do not think the Academy or the Army is the place for him."[36]

Rhodes was not among those in the class of 1889 who had grown to acknowledge and respect Young's strength of character and treat him "with the kindness and consideration which had long been his due." Rhodes's use of the term "darkey" showed him to be as small-minded and bigoted as he was when he first referred to Young in his June 1885 letter. His opinion that the academy and the army were no place for Young, despite his five hard years of work to earn his diploma and commission, exposed Rhodes as an unreformed racist.

It is unfortunate that the actions and words of Young's small circle of friends were not recorded. Had they been, they probably would have been full of understanding, support, and friendship. Certainly Skerrett, Bethel, Piper, Webster, McGlachlin, Harrison, Langhorne, Haan, and Bandholtz took the time to shake his hand, wish him good luck, and bid him farewell until a next meeting at some future army post. Perhaps Schermerhorn and Lamblin, former members of the class of 1889, were on hand for the graduation and also wished Young well.

Graduation

The official graduation speaker the summer of 1889 was Sen. Cushman K. Davis from Minnesota. Cushman had served during the Civil War as a lieutenant in the Twenty-eighth Wisconsin Volunteer Regiment, but more importantly, he was a member of the West Point Board of Visitors. His speech must not have been memorable, since none of the members of the class of 1889 mentioned it in their memoirs. They did, however, mention the antics and speeches of Gen. William T. Sherman.

The day before graduation, the day of the "last parade," Rhodes recounted that "General William Tecumseh Sherman, sitting on the hotel porch, expressed his fixed opinion that the cadet-girls were getting prettier every year; and addressing himself to a nearby graduate in gray, said: 'My boy, if you have not yet, picked out your girl, wait! They'll be all the prettier, next year!'"[37]

Rhodes remembered graduation day, June 12, 1889, in detail. He set the stage as follows: "In those hectic, early hours, busy hands were packing up, or attempting to settle money accounts with 'Old Spurge' [Capt. William F. Spurgin, treasurer]. And then, the first tap of the ten o'clock drum, brought graduates from the barracks 'with a rush,'—as is duly recorded in the *New York Tribune* of the day. And to the air of 'Auld Lang Syne,' '89 marched to the front of the old library, where over a thousand spectators were assembled to do them honor."[38]

Although General Sherman had promised cadets the day before that he would not give a speech, he could not resist the temptation. William Harts, who graduated fifth in the class of 1889, remembered Sherman's antics: "On graduation we were all handed our diplomas by General W. T. Sherman, one of my early heroes. He had written out an address but had forgotten his glasses. He said he would have to give us a talk instead." Harts continued: "I remember but little of what he said but only one anecdote remains in my memory. He said that once a young man came to him to get his help to enter West Point. The boy said that if he could get an appointment he would be one of the best in the class, never swear, drink or chew, he would get no demerits, stand one in his class, go to prayer-meetings and be a model boy. Sherman said, I turned to him and said, 'You damned little fool, do you think they make soldiers out of that kind of material?' This reply delighted all of us."[39]

Young must have been present in the audience for graduation, since it was a command performance for the corps. But instead of assembling with his graduating classmates, he sat with the other three classes as a spectator rather than a participant. He had looked forward to being handed his diploma by General Sherman, an officer and gentleman from his home state of Ohio, but instead he watched as his forty-eight classmates were presented their diplomas and then, one by one, departed West Point for their new assignments.[40]

34. Cadets marching in New York City
in April 1889 for the Centennial Parade
(Author's collection)

35. Delamere Skerrett, 1889
(West Point Library Special Collections)

36. Alexander R. Piper, 1889
(West Point Library Special Collections)

37. Walter A. Bethel, 1889
(West Point Library Special Collections)

38. George T. Langhorne, 1889
(West Point Library Special Collections)

39. Fisticuffs at West Point from a 1901 edition of *Harper's Weekly* (West Point Library Special Collections)

40. Maj. Gen. George W. Goethals (West Point Library Special Collections)

41. Class crest of the West Point class of 1889 (West Point Library Special Collections)

42. Painting of 2nd Lt. Charles Young by J. W. Shannon
(Courtesy of the National Afro-American Museum and Cultural
Center, Wilberforce OH)

Young's Summer

Although the academic board declared Young deficient in engineering, it recommended that he "be allowed to remain at the Academy for the purpose of making up his deficiency." This was not an unusual occurrence, as in the prior three years at least one first classmen from each graduating class had been held past graduation for disciplinary or academic reasons, but the board's process of making this decision was anything but usual. On June 8, 1889, the board met pursuant to the call of the superintendent. "The assistant professor of Engineering [Goethals] then took his seat on the Board" and they considered Young's case. After discussion, "The Question was then put: Is Cadet Young deficient in Engineering? Upon which vote was Ayes 8, Noes 4, absent 1, Decision, affirmative." Young's diploma and commission hung in the balance.[41]

After some parliamentary wrangling, a motion "that Cadet Young be recommended to the Secretary of War for discharge" carried. No vote count was listed. After further discussion, a move carried "that recommendation be made to the Sec[retary of] War that Cadet Young be allowed to remain at the Academy for the purpose of making up his deficiency in Engineering to the satisfaction of the Academic Board on or before Sept. 1, 1889." Young had his stay.[42]

Lieutenant Goethals devoted two summer months of special tutoring to enable Young to pass the required reexamination in civil and military engineering. "My sympathies were aroused," Goethals admitted, "and I offered to give him a certain amount of time daily in order to assist him in preparation for the examination which he was to take the last of August." Young acknowledged Goethals's "disinterested help" in his Liberia letter. It must have been a difficult situation for both men, since Young showed little aptitude in engineering and Goethals was brilliant in the field.[43]

This man who took special interest in Young, giving him his "last chance," deserves a closer look. George Washington Goethals was born to Flemish parents in Brooklyn in 1858. He won an appointment to West Point from a local congressman, graduated second in his class in 1880, and was commissioned in the Corps of Engineers. He returned twice to West Point as an instructor between assignments on various rivers and the Atlantic Coast building bridges, improving navigation, and completing fortifications. He was most celebrated for serving as the chief engineer on the Panama Canal project, which began in 1907 and was completed six months ahead of schedule in 1914. It was the grandest engineering feat of his generation. [44]

In preparing Young for his makeup examination, Goethals accomplished his final mission at West Point. He departed the academy on August 28, 1889, for an assignment building locks and dams along the Tennessee and Cumberland rivers. When it reconvened on August 31, 1889, the academic board found that Young was no longer deficient in engineering and recommended him for commissioning in the cavalry or infantry. Young graduated on August 31, ten weeks after his classmates. It is unlikely that any fanfare accompanied his graduation day, and he certainly took no pleasure in being the class immortal. [45]

Assignment Troubles

The army commissioned Young an additional second lieutenant in the Tenth U.S. Cavalry on September 14, 1889. [46] Unwritten army policy dictated that Young be assigned to a black regiment, as had Flipper and Alexander before him. In acknowledging his appointment to the adjutant general in Washington, Young gave notice that he would be spending home leave at his parents' home in Zanesville, Ohio. At the end of his graduation leave of absence in November, Young looked forward to joining his regiment and embarking on his career. But controversy concerning his race and assignment began even before he reported to his new duty station. [47]

While Young was on leave, the War Department informed him that he had been reassigned to the Twenty-fifth U.S. Infantry, also a black unit, because of a vacancy in that regiment. Young protested the change in an October 1889 letter to the adjutant general, stating that he had already made arrangements to secure a cavalry uniform and that any change would be expensive. He also declared that he was fond of horses and was confident that he would be a successful cavalry officer. The adjutant general responded that Young's request would be considered and that his application for transfer would be reviewed if a vacancy opened for a second lieutenant in the Ninth or Tenth Cavalry.[48]

A happy Young received a telegram on October 29, 1889, from Washington asking if he would accept a transfer to the Ninth U.S. Cavalry. A handwritten note in the adjutant general's files stated the reason for this vacancy: "Lt. Young, the colored graduate, can now be re-transferred to the Cavalry—the death of Lt. Humphrey making a vacancy in the 9th Regt." Lt. B. S. Humphrey, Ninth U.S. Cavalry, had died of a heart attack while on hunting leave. Young wasted no time and cabled the War Department his acceptance the following day. On October 31 the War Department issued special orders transferring Young from the Twenty-fifth Infantry to the Ninth Cavalry. He never served in either the Tenth Cavalry or Twenty-fifth Infantry during this time. Young had his cavalry assignment, but the storm of controversy was not over.[49]

Maj. Guy V. Henry, acting commander of the Ninth U.S. Cavalry, protested to the War Department about Young's assignment.[50] The regiment already had Young's former West Point roommate, 2nd Lt. John Alexander, assigned to the unit, and Henry feared that the presence of a second black line officer in the Ninth Cavalry would "be detrimental to the good of the regiment. . . . by causing officers not to apply for assignment to the regiment." In his letter he stated: "If this transfer was made in order that Lt. Alexander might have company it has failed, for in a letter from an officer I am informed that Lieutenant Alexander objects to Lt. Young's assignment, as keeping them together gives no benefit to their efforts to advance their race."[51]

To be fair, Major Henry, a grizzled veteran of many campaigns, was acting in what he thought were the regiment's best interests. Henry, who had been made a brevet brigadier general twice for gallant and meritorious service—once as a volunteer during the Civil War, when he earned a Medal of Honor, and later as a Regular fighting the Sioux—had worked for years to raise the reputation of the Ninth Cavalry as an elite regiment to attract the best and brightest officers. He bore Young no ill will, but he recognized the attitude of many in the officer corps. To him this request was not about race but about regimental reputation.[52]

The War Department's response to Major Henry's protest revealed the real reason for Young's rapid change in assignments. The adjutant general summarized the process as follows: "It will be remembered that Lt. Young was first assigned as an *additional* [second lieutenant] in the 10th Cavalry; that when in that position he was liable (as the senior Cavalry additional) to have a vacancy fall to him in a *white* regiment at any moment; that to avoid this he was appointed to a vacancy in the 25th Infantry (the Secty, having decided he should be in a colored regiment) and that, as Young had purchased a *Cavalry* uniform, and wanted cavalry, he was transferred to the first vacancy in a colored Cav regiment, which happened to be *the 9th*, and he has *now been confirmed by the Senate, and commissioned in the 9th*."[53] In short, the adjutant general had moved Young quickly to the Twenty-fifth Infantry and, finally, to the Ninth Cavalry to avoid the possibility of Young's going to a white cavalry unit to command white enlisted soldiers. In a black regiment, Young would work side by side with white officers but command only black troops. To the War Department this was the lesser of two evils, but to Young it was a harbinger of troubles to come.

For Young, overcoming this final hurdle meant that his West Point struggles were finally coming to an end. After five years and five months, he had his coveted diploma as well as his commission as a second lieutenant in the Ninth U.S. Cavalry. His first duty assignment was Fort Robinson, Nebraska, where his classmate and friend Alexander Piper was also posted, though to a different regiment. At Fort Robinson, the next struggle for recognition and acceptance in the U.S. Army began, one that would be longer and more difficult than at West Point. But that is another story.

Epilogue

Reflections

> No man ever more truly deserved the high repute in
> which he was held. He overcame prejudice which would
> have discouraged many lesser men.
>
> THEODORE ROOSEVELT JR.

In 1915, more than a quarter of a century after he graduated from West Point, Col. Charles Young reflected on his time there in a letter to a friend and classmate, Col. Delamere Skerrett. He wrote the letter from Monrovia, Liberia, where he was posted as the military attaché. The letter was heartfelt and telling.

Monrovia, Liberia
Africa, 23 July, 1915
My dear Skerrett:

It is a long hike to you from a camp in the jungle of Liberia
where I'm trying on nothing save a rice bag (to give the soldier's
"chop") to make a road from the Capital Monrovia, through the
"big bush" to the hinterland. I find that the coast has done all it
can for the country and that if it ever is going to be developed
and saved to my people we must get to the native man in the
interior and on the hinterland.

1. The Frontier Forces organized, 2. A Map of the Country
made for them, 3. I got myself this final task prior to yielding myself to the Manchu Law next year—But this is not at all what I
started out to write about. It was that I desired to thank you and
Bethel for remembering me at the Class dinner last year at the
Point, and sending me the Menu Card and the other literary dope

pertaining to the Reunion—I also shall write to Schermerhorn and Piper, the former for the thanks I owe him for the very interesting brochure of the occasion which he kindly sent; the latter for the repeated letters with which he plies me in vain.

You know for me the Academy has, even to this day, heartaches in spite of the many advantages I derived there. The sole bright things that come to my heart are the friendship and sympathy from men like you, Bethel, Webster, McGlachlin, Harrison, Lamblin, Langhorne, Barnum, and Bandholtz. Yes, I must mention the disinterested help of Col. W. B. Gordon and General Goethals—I can never forget them; and have tried to pass along to others the kindness of you all, both in America, the Philippines, the West Indies and Africa. So you see you can not always tell the wide reaching influence of a word of cheer to even a black man. God knows how many white ones I have helped because you all helped me. Simply trying to pay the interest on the debt of gratitude, I owe you, that's all. The world is better and only worth living perhaps, because it has its Skerretts, Bethels, Goethals, Gordons, Barnums, Haans and Langhornes with the others of that stripe. May they live long.

With grateful esteem,
Yours sincere,
Chas. Young[1]

This fascinating letter opens a window on Young's deepest feelings about his years at West Point. First and foremost, the experience was tremendously painful for him, leaving wounds that had not healed twenty-five years later. Despite the painful memories of his five years at West Point, Young remembered the goodwill and kindness shown him by a small group of cadets. He was touched by the recent contact made by four of his classmates and remembered the compassion and civility shown by several other cadets and professors.

All of the individuals named in this letter have been discussed in the preceding chapters, but it is useful to review whom Young thought worthy of note and why. He mentioned by name ten members of his class of 1889: Skerrett, Bethel, Schermerhorn, Piper, Webster, McGlachlin, Harrison, Lamblin, Langhorne, and Haan. Of these, Schermerhorn and Lamblin did not graduate. Young also noted one upperclassman, Malvern-Hill Barnum, class of 1886, and one underclassman, Harry Bandholtz, class of 1890. Lastly, he noted the "disinterested help" of William Gordon and George Goethals, both assistant professors and first lieutenants at the time. Gordon taught physics, and Goethals was the engineering instructor who flunked and then tutored Young at the end of his firstie year.

At first glance, the number of classmates whom Young considers friends seems high—eight out of forty-nine in his graduating class, or roughly one in six.[2] But these relationships likely developed gradually over the four years he spent with his class and deepened toward the end, when his determination earned the grudging admiration of even his harshest enemies. Some of these friendships likely grew and expanded in the years after West Point, as these officers served together in the Regular Army. Harrison, Skerrett, and Piper served on the western frontier at the same time as Young, while Haan, McGlachlin, Langhorne, and Webster served in the Philippines while he was there.

Also revealing are those missing from the list. Young never mentions any friends in his original class of 1888, including those who began their cadet careers in 1884 with Young and were turned back and repeated a year with him. Four of the five cadets who were turned back with him his plebe year also graduated with him in 1889: Graves, Normoyle, Leitch, and Barrios. It is somewhat surprising that he did not form a bond with any of those who shared the same five-year trial as he.

Three days after writing to Skerrett, Young penned a similar letter to his friend Alexander Piper:

Capt. Alexander Piper
Brooklyn, New York
Dear Capt. Piper:

I've got "a late"—an inexcusable late so much so that an absence total and cold would be far better than trying to get into line, if

I did not desire to thank you for the letters you sent me regarding the Class Dinner and Reunion at the Point. Your first letter passed me on the high seas, where I was going home in search of health from this terrible Black Water Fever of the West Coast. Your second letter reached me at my home trying to recuperate but far from being able to handle a pen. I thought to answer afterward and tell you how Liberia called again to duty—it was mislaid and then forgot; then I returned and into the boiling pot of hard work I was immediately forced. Indeed, the Brochure setting forth the transaction both in New York and West Point, and sent me by Schermerhorn, meets me in the jungle about 75 miles from Monrovia, making a road thru the said jungle to the hinterland, to help in some permanent work here for my people before the Manchu Law calls me back to duty with our own troops in the U.S Army.

We have succeeded in organizing a decent Frontier Force, in making a working system of Reports, Returns, and Regulations, a Map of the Republic, and when this road of possibly 10 miles is finished with a Central Mil[itary] Station at its further end my work I laid out at the Army War College before coming over here will be finished. The American officers that I brought here with me have been loyal and worked well. The troops are natives, not Liberians. They are not one whit inferior in the soldier spirit to our best black troops in our own Army, which as you know is saying much.

But I set out to thank you all, of the Class who remembered me, both while getting up the Reunion, during and since.

While West Point was pretty hard pulling for me, still the roughness was relieved by the sympathy of many of my classmates, to whom I shall ever be grateful and among I shall remember you.

Chas. Young[3]

Young's letters from the jungles of Liberia come as close as anything to revealing his true feelings about his West Point experience. The official academic and disciplinary records reflect a constant struggle to keep his head above water. Most of this he did alone, relying on his own sense of duty, focused determination, and strength of character.

During his first three years Young had the critical support and counsel of John Alexander, the importance of which cannot be overemphasized. But in his early years, at least, he did not have the support and comradeship of his white classmates. Perhaps the absence of the Alexander's counsel and friendship during his last two years at the academy caused Young to reach out to his white classmates.

Toward the end of his five-year ordeal, a small band in his class demonstrated forthrightness and moral courage in publicly acknowledging their admiration and friendship for Young. In some cases this may have amounted to no more than a subtle offer of encouragement or a private show of support. In other cases, such as with Skerrett, McGlachlin, and Piper, their considerable time spent together led to real friendship and understanding. Young certainly deserved all of their respect for his accomplishments over five difficult years, but it was not a given in those days that he would be accorded anything but scorn or indifference from his white classmates.

As revealed in his letters, Young chose the high road. He could not forget his difficult years at West Point, in spite of the advantages he gained by graduating from one of the premier military academies in the world and one of the best technical schools in the United States. But the essential experience he took away from his time there was the friendship and kindness shown by a small band of classmates. And this he passed along in kind to countless others during a long and successful career in the Regular Army. For him it made life worth living, and made his country worth serving.

Young wrote his Liberia letters in 1915, when his reputation and career in the army were on the rise, despite his race. In less than a year he would chase Pancho Villa with Brig. Gen. John Pershing in Mexico, command a squadron of the Tenth U.S. Cavalry, and be promoted to lieutenant colonel in the field by his former cadet first captain. During the campaign in Mexico, Pershing was impressed by Young's leadership and decisiveness and placed his name on a short list of officers he recommended to command brigades in the coming war in Europe.[4]

Young's good fortune did not last, however. Serious medical problems discovered on the eve of the U.S. entry into World War I prevented him from becoming the first African American general. Instead, in 1917 he was medically retired, promoted to colonel, and sent home to Ohio. Young never lived out his dream of leading black troops in combat in France; instead, he was recalled to active duty with the Ohio National Guard after the war to do meaningless staff work. A bitter and angry Colonel Young wrote the following letter on January 15, 1919, to a young African American seeking his advice on attending the academy:

> My dear Mr. Smith:
>
> I have your letter of the 26th in which you ask my advice as to your future course in going to a Military Academy. My advice is, don't think of it. If you put one-half of the time, patience, diligence and "pep" in any other profession or vocation, you will succeed and get rich but if you go thru the Military Academy it means a dog's life while you are there and for years after you graduate, a pittance of a salary as a subaltern and in the end retirement on a mere competence, which does not pay if you have a little girl in view that wishes to wear diamonds.
>
> I tell you this as a brother who has been over the whole road. I wish I had taken my time and put it in tropical agriculture and supplement it with the Spanish language and I would have been a rich man now instead of a Colonel on the scrap heap of the U. S. Army.
>
> Very sincerely yours,
> CHAS. YOUNG
> COLONEL, U.S. ARMY
> COMMANDING[5]

Young was embittered as a result of what he perceived as a premature and unfair forced retirement in 1917. In 1915 he had described the heartaches he had experienced at the academy but also the many advantages he derived. In 1919, in contrast, he advised his correspondent against attendance, warning of a "dog's life" at West Point and a pitiful carrier in the army thereafter. Although he did not say so in his Liberia letter, Young gave the impression he would attend West Point again if given the chance. Not so in the 1919 letter.

But in the end, Young again answered the call of duty he learned perhaps better than any of his classmates at West Point. Duty to country mattered more to Colonel Young than did the life and riches he mentioned in his note to Smith. He acknowledged this in a February 17, 1919, letter to his friend Alexander Piper, who was the scribe of the class of 1889. He wrote Piper in response to an invitation he received to the thirtieth-anniversary reunion of their class. He had been invited to the reunions before but had never attended:

> My dear Piper:
>
> I received your Mess Call for the 30th Anniversary and if I am not on Fatigue in Hayti or Africa I shall surely come this time. I have promised the Secretary of State to go to Africa and there is also a call to Hayti again, so you see that I do not belong to myself wholly in spite of being a Colonel on the Retired list.
>
> With heartiest good wishes for you,
> Your friend and classmate,
> *Young*[6]

Young missed the class of 1889 reunion in 1919 preparing for his Liberia departure. He had accepted a request from the U.S. secretary of state, Robert Lansing, and the president of Liberia, Daniel Howard, to return to Monrovia for a second tour of duty as military attaché to complete the work he had begun seven years earlier. He did so against the advice of his friend W. E. B. DuBois, who knew the danger the assignment posed to Young's health. Young knew the risks he faced. He wrote prophetically in 1918 to Sen. Atlee Pomerene of Ohio: "You must confess that no man has greater love than to die for the thing he espouses. My father died of complications brought on by exposure in the War of the Rebellion. The heritage of honor left me by him as a private solder . . . I have tried to add to as an officer for my family and race and not to tarnish."[7]

Sadly, Young never again had an opportunity to attend another gathering of his classmates. He died two years later, on January 8, 1922, while on an intelligence mission in Lagos, Nigeria, succumbing to the illnesses he had been exposed to during his earlier Africa service. He was buried by the British in Lagos and later was interred with full military honors in 1923 by the U.S. Army in Arlington National Cemetery.

It was a sad ending to a journey that had begun nearly sixty years earlier in the slave quarters of a log house in Kentucky. Young had traveled far since leaving his father and mother in Ripley to take on the challenges of West Point, a white bastion of the military establishment on the Hudson. His army career took him all over the United States, the Philippines, the West Indies, and Africa. But he lived and died embodying the motto of "Duty, Honor, Country" he learned so well at the academy.

Young succeeded where so many others had failed, and he was the third and last African American to graduate from West Point in the nineteenth century. But his importance is greater. Unlike the two black academy graduates before him, Young went on to a long and distinguished career in the military and achieved the rank of colonel. After him, racial intolerance closed the door to blacks at the academy, and another half century passed before another African American graduated from West Point. Young was not alive to see Benjamin O. Davis Jr. graduate in 1936, but he had passed the torch to another generation of black West Pointers.

Appendix

Class of 1889

From *Register of Graduates* (2000), p. 4–64.

Admitted as cadets: 7 in 1884; 33 on June 14, 1885; 9 on September 1, 1885

Graduated on June 12, 1889

Antonio Barrios: born in Guatemala; admitted as foreign cadet; first foreign cadet to graduate from West Point; minister of public works in Guatemala; died in Guatemala in 1915, age forty-nine. (Cullum no. 3329, 48th in class)

Morris Keene Barroll: born in and admitted from Maryland; selected Artillery; retired as colonel in 1920; died in Washington DC in 1947, age eighty-one. (Cullum no. 3298, 17th in class)

Walter Augustus Bethel: born in and admitted from Ohio; selected Artillery; studied law; promoted to major general and appointed judge advocate general of the U.S. Army; retired disabled in 1924; died in Washington DC in 1954, age eighty-seven. (Cullum no. 3295, 14th in class)

Edmund Molyneux Blake: born in South Carolina; admitted from North Carolina; selected Artillery; retired as colonel in 1922; died in Washington DC in 1927, age sixty-one. (Cullum no. 3288, 7th in class)

Edwin Victor Bookmiller: born in and admitted from Ohio; selected Infantry; retired disabled as major in 1915; recalled to active duty in 1917–19 as colonel; died in Washington DC in 1946, age seventy-nine. (Cullum no. 3309, 28th in class)

Samuel Burkhardt Jr.: born in and admitted from Illinois; selected Infantry; Vera Cruz Expedition, 1914; retired as colonel in 1920; died in Chicago in 1929, age sixty-four. (Cullum no. 3326, 45th in class)

Archibald Campbell: born in Pennsylvania; admitted from New York; selected Artillery; retired as brigadier general in 1929; died in Virginia in 1959, age ninety-three. (Cullum no. 3302, 21st in class)

Sydney Amos Cloman: born in and admitted from Ohio; selected Infantry; observer of Russian Army, 1905; military attaché, London, 1907–11; resigned as major in 1917; colonel in National Army in 1917; retired as lieutenant colonel in 1919; promoted to colonel posthumously; died in California in 1923, age fifty-five. (Cullum no. 3321, 40th in class)

Edwin Tuttle Cole: born in Maryland; admitted from Pennsylvania; selected Infantry; retired in 1911 as major; recalled to active duty in 1911–19 as colonel; died in Pennsylvania in 1940, age seventy-three. (Cullum no. 3316, 35th in class)

Charles Crawford: born in Ohio; admitted from Kentucky; selected Infantry; promoted to brigadier general in World War I; retired disabled as colonel in 1919; retired as brigadier general in 1930, died in Kansas in 1945, age seventy-nine. (Cullum no. 3322, 41st in class)

Albert Milligan D'Armit: born in Pennsylvania; admitted from Iowa; selected Engineers; died as first lieutenant while an instructor at West Point in 1895, age thirty. (Cullum no. 3283, 2nd in class)

Wilmont Edward Ellis: Born in and admitted from New Jersey; selected Artillery; retired as colonel in 1920; died in South Carolina in 1938, age seventy. (Cullum no. 3291, 10th in class)

Clement A. Finley Flagler: born in Georgia; admitted from Iowa; selected Engineers; major general and Forty-second Division commander during World War I; died at Baltimore MD in 1922, age fifty-four. (Cullum no. 3284, 3rd in class)

William Sydney Graves: born in and admitted from Texas; selected Infantry; promoted to major general and commander of American Expeditionary Force, Siberia; retired in 1928; died in New Jersey in 1940, age seventy-four. (Cullum no. 3323, 42nd in class)

William George Haan: born in and admitted from Indiana; selected Artillery; major general and Thirty-second Division commander during World War I; retired in 1922; died in Washington DC in 1924, age sixty-one. (Cullum no. 3293, 12th in class)

Charles Baldwin Hagadorn: born in and admitted from New York; selected Infantry; died on active duty as colonel at Camp Grant IL in 1918, age fifty-two. (Cullum no. 3306, 25th in class)

John Power Hains: born in Pennsylvania; admitted at large; selected Artillery; retired as colonel in 1929; last surviving member of his class; died in Washington DC in 1964, age ninety-eight. (Cullum no. 3303, 22nd in class)

Chester Harding: born in Mississippi; admitted from Alabama; selected Engineers; governor of the Panama Canal Zone; retired as brigadier general in 1920; died in Massachusetts in 1936, age sixty-nine. (Cullum no. 3285, 4th in class)

Ralph Harrison: born in and admitted from Missouri; selected Cavalry; retired as colonel in 1926; died in California in 1933, age sixty-seven. (Cullum no. 3299, 18th in class)

William Wright Harts: born in and admitted from Illinois; selected Engineers; construction engineer for the Lincoln Memorial and aide to President Wilson, 1913–17; retired as brigadier general in 1930; died in Connecticut in 1961, age ninety-four. (Cullum no. 3286, 5th in class)

George LeRoy Irwin: born in Michigan; admitted from Illinois; selected Artillery; retired as major general in 1928; died in Trinidad in 1931, age sixty-two. (Cullum no. 3305, 24th in class)

Ben Johnson: born in and appointed from Mississippi; selected Artillery; resigned in 1889; construction superintendent of the Gatun Locks, Panama Canal; died in Mississippi in 1940, age seventy-four. (Cullum no. 3297, 16th in class)

Sidney Sauzade Jordan: born in and admitted from New

Jersey; selected Artillery; retired disabled as lieutenant colonel, 1915; recalled to active duty as colonel, 1917–19; died in Washington DC in 1944, age seventy-six. (Cullum no. 3294, 13th in class)

Ulysses Grant Kemp: born in and admitted from Ohio; selected Cavalry; died on active duty as first lieutenant at Fort Grant AZ in 1898, age thirty-two. (Cullum no. 3314, 33rd in class)

William Lacy Kenly: born in and admitted from Maryland; selected Artillery; aide to General McArthur, 1900–1901; major general and director of Military Aeronautics during World War I; retired in 1919; died in Washington DC in 1928, age sixty-three. (Cullum no. 3292, 11th in class)

George William Kirkman: born in Texas; admitted from Illinois; selected Infantry; dismissed in 1900; reappointed by act of Congress in 1900; dismissed in 1905 as captain. (Cullum no. 3319, 38th in class)

Francis Edmond Lacey Jr.: born in West Virginia; appointed from Michigan; selected Infantry; retired as colonel in 1922; died in Connecticut in 1925, age fifty-seven. (Cullum no. 3320, 39th in class)

George Tayloe Langhorne: born in Kentucky; admitted from Virginia; selected Cavalry; military attaché to Brussels, 1897–98, and Berlin, 1913–15; retired as colonel in 1931; died in Chicago in 1962, age ninety-four. (Cullum no. 3313, 32nd in class)

William Lassiter: born in and admitted from Virginia; selected Artillery; military attaché to London, 1916–17; promoted to major general and Thirty-second Division commander during World War I; retired in 1931; died in California in 1959, age ninety-one. (Cullum no. 3304, 23rd in class)

Harry Raymond Lee: born in and admitted from Rhode Island; selected Infantry; retired as colonel in 1922; died in Washington DC in 1949, age eighty-two. (Cullum no. 3308, 27th in class)

Joseph Dugald Leitch: born in Michigan; admitted from Nebraska; selected Infantry; promoted to major general and chief of staff of American Expeditionary Force, Siberia; retired in 1928; died in California in 1938, age seventy-four. (Cullum no. 3325, 44th in class)

John Thomas Martin: born in and admitted from Ohio; selected Artillery; died en route from Philippines at sea in 1906, age forty. (Cullum no. 3289, 8th in class)

Edward Fenton McGlachlin Jr.: born in and admitted from Wisconsin; selected Artillery; promoted to major general and First Division commander during World War I; retired in 1923; died in Washington DC in 1946, age seventy-eight. (Cullum no. 3301, 20th in class)

Robert McGregor: born in and admitted from Michigan; selected Engineers; died as captain while city engineer in Manila in 1902, age thirty-eight. (Cullum no. 3287, 6th in class)

James Edward Normoyle: born in Michigan; admitted from Illinois; selected Infantry; quartermaster of the Yellow Fever Camps in Cuba, 1898–1900; died on active duty as major at Fort Ontario NY in 1916, age fifty. (Cullum no. 3327, 46th in class)

Matt Ransom Peterson: born in and admitted from North Carolina; selected Infantry; died on active duty of yellow fever in Havana in 1900, age thirty-four. (Cullum no. 3315, 34th in class)

William Allen Phillips: born in Texas; admitted from Tennessee; selected Infantry; resigned 1915; reappointed 1916; retired disabled as colonel in 1921; died in Maryland in 1925, age fifty-nine. (Cullum no. 3317, 36th in class)

Alexander Ross Piper: born in New York; admitted from Idaho Territory; selected Infantry; retired disabled as captain in 1899; recalled to active duty, 1917–19; retired as colonel in 1919; president of the Association of Graduates 1934–36; died in New York in 1952, age eighty-seven. (Cullum no. 3310, 29th in class)

Charles Dudley Rhodes: born in and admitted from Ohio;

selected Cavalry; promoted to major general and Forty-second and Thirty-fourth Division commander in World War I; retired in 1928; died in Washington DC in 1948, age eighty-two. (Cullum no. 3307, 26th in class)

Delamere Skerrett: born in Ohio; admitted from New York; selected Artillery; retired as colonel in 1918; died in New York in 1939, age seventy-three. (Cullum no. 3300, 19th in class)

Edward Villeroy Stockham: born in and admitted from New Jersey; selected Infantry; resigned in 1889; served as captain in World War I; honorably discharged as major in 1919; died in Maryland in 1932, age sixty-eight. (Cullum no. 3328, 47th in class)

Alvin Humphrey Sydenham: born in Iowa; admitted from Nebraska; selected Cavalry; died on active duty as a second lieutenant at Fort Canby WA in 1893, age twenty-six. (Cullum no. 3296, 15th in class)

John Rogers Meigs Taylor: born in Washington DC; admitted at large; selected Infantry; military attaché to Turkey, 1911–14; retired disabled in 1914; recalled to active duty, 1914–19; retired as colonel in 1918; died in Washington DC in 1949, age eighty-four. (Cullum no. 3318, 37th in class)

Frank Daniel Webster: born in and admitted from Missouri; selected Infantry; promoted to brigadier general in World War I; retired disabled as colonel in 1918; retired as brigadier general in 1930; died in Kansas in 1932, age sixty-five. (Cullum no. 3324, 43rd in class)

Francis Wallace Willcox: born in and admitted from Tennessee; selected Artillery; resigned in 1891; died in New York City in 1925, age fifty-eight. (Cullum no. 3290, 9th in class)

Eben Eveleth Winslow: born in Washington DC; admitted from Massachusetts; selected Engineers; retired as colonel in 1922; promoted posthumously to brigadier general; died in Tennessee in 1928, age sixty-two. (Cullum no. 3282, 1st in class)

Edward Thomas Winston: born in and admitted from Tennessee; selected Infantry; retired disabled as captain in 1901;

active duty, 1902; retired as lieutenant colonel in 1921; died in Georgia in 1923, age fifty-nine. (Cullum no. 3311, 30th in class)

Winthrop Samuel Wood: born in Washington DC; admitted from Maine; selected Cavalry; retired as brigadier general in 1929; died in Washington DC in 1937, age seventy-one. (Cullum no. 3312, 31st in class)

Charles Young: born in Kentucky; admitted from Ohio; selected Cavalry; military attaché to Haiti, 1904–7, and Liberia, 1912–15; Punitive Expedition to Mexico; retired disabled in 1917 and promoted to colonel; recalled to active duty in 1918; military attaché to Liberia, 1919–22; died on active duty on intelligence mission in Nigeria in 1919, age fifty-seven. (Cullum no. 3330, 49th in class)

General officers: 17 (1 posthumously)

Died on active duty: 9

Retired disabled/medical: 10

Recalled to active duty: 11

Notes

Abbreviations

ACP Appointment, Commission, and Personal Branch of the Adjutant General's Office

MCM Mason County Museum, Maysville KY

NAAMCC National Afro-American Museum and Cultural Center, Wilber-force OH

NARA National Archives and Records Administration, College Park MD

USMA United States Military Academy

UTPL Union Township Public Library, Ripley OH

WPLSC West Point Library Special Collections, West Point NY

WRHS Western Reserve Historical Society, Cleveland OH

Prologue

1. Charles Young to Delamere Skerrett, July 23, 1915, Charles Young Papers, WPLSC.

Enslaved in Kentucky

1. Arminta Bruen's name is spelled several different ways in the records. In the census of 1870 it is spelled Arminta, and in the census of 1880 it is spelled Armenta. Children called her Aunt Mintie. Her own children addressed letters to her later as Arminta, so I have used that spelling. Likewise, her last name has been spelled Bruin and Bruen.

2. Grant, *Personal Memoirs*, 405; Charles Noel Young, "Biography of Col. Charles Young," n.d., Charles Young Papers, Coleman Collection, Akron OH. This incomplete draft of a biography by Young's son Charles Noel Young was written sometime in the 1950s as a continuation of an effort begun by Young's widow, Ada, after his death. The biography is full of errors but is valuable for the family stories it relates. Some of these recollections probably have some kern of truth in them, but they have to be reconciled with official records wherever possible.

3. David Gray, interview by the author, Ripley OH, May 1, 2003. Some sources have incorrectly listed the place of Charles Young's birth as Hildreth Plantation. The cabin where Young was born still stands on what is now called Rushmeyer farm. It was formally known as Hildreth farm when it belonged to William Hildreth, a descendant of the Willetts. David and Jan

Loney now own the property, and the cabin still stands. It is on Helena Road not far from the old railroad station.

4. Calvert and Klee, *The Towns of Mason County*, 63; Harrison, *The Civil War in Kentucky*, 2.

5. Wright, "Afro-Americans," 3–5; Klotter, *Our Kentucky*, 106–110; Fields, *Slavery and Freedom*, 2.

6. Klotter, *Our Kentucky*, 111–112; "Kentucky and the Question of Slavery," http://www.ket.org/underground/history/questionsof.htm.

7. Miller, *Slavery in Mason County*, 2:214–20.

8. C. N. Young, "Biography of Col. Charles Young."

9. "Charles Young: The Desert and Solitary Place," Young Papers, Coleman Collection. This undated short biography of Young was found with the notes and drafts of Charles N. Young. It contains more errors and is written in a different style, but it has many of the same stories as the draft by Charles N. Young. It may have been written by Ada Young.

10. Fox-Genovese, *Within the Plantation Household*, 174–75.

11. Calvert and Klee, *The Towns of Mason County*, 63; Lynn David, researcher, MCM, e-mail, July 5, 2003; C. N. Young, "Biography of Col. Charles Young."

12. Fox-Genovese, *Within the Plantation Household*, 146.

13. Frederic, *Slave Life in Virginia and Kentucky*, 14–61.

14. Stuckey, "Through the Prism of Folklore," 134–47; DuBois quote on 134.

15. Frederic, *Slave Life in Virginia and Kentucky*, 95–109.

16. Wright, "Afro-Americans," 3–5. According to Wright, "Ownership of slaves was profitable to Kentucky whites; the slave trade shipped approximately 80,000 Africans southward between 1830 and 1860" (4).

17. Frederic, *Slave Life in Virginia and Kentucky*, 41–43.

18. Miller, *Slavery in Mason County*, 1:129.

19. May's Lick Baptist Church Record, n.d., 115, MCM; undated article from the *Maysville (KY) Daily Bulletin*, MCM.

20. Greene, *Early Life of Colonel Charles Young*, 7. Deacon Allen Bowlden of the Maysville Second Baptist Church confirmed that Reverend Markam was the pastor of the church at this time. C. N. Young, "Biography of Col. Charles Young."

21. Frederic, *Slave Life in Virginia and Kentucky*, 32–35; Lynn David, researcher, MCM, e-mail, July 5, 2003; Shaffer, "In the Shadow of the Old Constitution," 59–64.

22. Harrison, *The Civil War in Kentucky*, 1–57.

23. Meier and Rudwick, *From Plantation to Ghetto*, 142–45.

24. Harrison, *The Civil War in Kentucky*, 91; Berlin, *Freedom*, 14.

25. Harrison, *The Civil War in Kentucky*, 89-91.

26. *Maysville (KY) Bulletin*, September 21, 1865.

27. Col. Charles Young to Sen. Atlee Pomerene, August 20, 1918, Young Papers, Coleman Collection; C. N. Young, "Biography of Col. Charles Young."

28. Fields, *Slavery and Freedom*, 125; Berlin, *Freedom*, 275-78.

29. C. N. Young, "Biography of Col. Charles Young."

30. Summary of Units and Miscellaneous Service Cards, 5th U.S. Colored Heavy Artillery, microfilm series M1818, roll 108, NARA.

31. Civil War Soldiers and Sailors System, National Park Service, www.nara.gov/education/teaching/usct; Frederick H. Dyer, *A Compendium of the War of the Rebellion*, M1818, roll 108, NARA.

32. C. N. Young, "Biography of Col. Charles Young"; Civil War Soldiers and Sailors System, National Park Service, www.nara.gov/education/teaching/usct; Dyer, *A Compendium of the War of the Rebellion*; Heitman, *Historical Register*, 2:598-601.

33. Berlin et al., *Slaves No More*, 224.

34. Discharge certificate of Pvt. Gabriel Young, Young Papers, Coleman Collection.

35. Summary of Units and Miscellaneous Service Cards, 5th U.S. Colored Heavy Artillery, microfilm series M1818, roll 108, NARA.

36. *Maysville (KY) Bulletin*, September 21, 1865.

37. Fields, *Slavery and Freedom*, 91, 167-93; Berlin et al., *Slaves No More*, 74.

38. Fields, *Slavery and Freedom*, 167-93.

39. In Charles Young's acknowledgment of his appointment to West Point, dated May 10, 1884, he lists his age at twenty years and two months and his period of residency in Ohio as nineteen years and no months. Nomination file of Charles Young, War Department Records, NARA.

Freedom in Ohio

1. U.S. Census of 1870, Inhabitants of Huntington Township, County of Brown, State of Ohio, August 12, 1870, courtesy of UTPL.

2. C. N. Young, "Biography of Col. Charles Young"; "The Desert and Solitary Place."

3. C. N. Young, "Biography of Col. Charles Young"; Charles Young to Arminta Young, May 11, 1919, Young Papers, Coleman Collection. Slickaway and Porter's Place are all in the general area of where Gabriel Young lived during the 1870 census.

4. Census of 1870; Gladstone, *Men of Color*, 97. Gabriel's year of birth is indicated in the 1870 census as 1838, in his Union army enlistment papers as 1840, and in the 1880 census as 1842.

5. Census of 1870.

6. Gray, interview.

7. Census of 1870. Peter Young is listed as a mulatto, a term then used to describe a person of mixed white and black ancestry. In this book I refer to mulattos as blacks or African Americans, since the term *mulatto* is no longer used.

8. Census of 1870. Charles Young is listed as seven years old at his last birthday. Since he was born on March 12, 1864, he should have been listed as six years old at this time. Ten years later, in the June 1880 census, he is correctly listed as sixteen.

9. Berlin et al., *Slaves No More*, 224.

10. C. N. Young, "Biography of Col. Charles Young"; "Charles Young: The Desert and Solitary Place"; Broadstone, *History of Greene County*, 948.

11. Sprague, *His Promised Land*, 25–70.

12. "Charles Young: The Desert and Solitary Place."

13. Pension Files, 1861–1934, microfilm publication T288, roll 542, NARA.

14. Hagedorn, *Beyond the River*, 9–10, 43.

15. Hagedorn, *Beyond the River*, 12–13.

16. Hagedorn, *Beyond the River*, 34–35, 51, 99.

17. Hagedorn, *Beyond the River*, 34–35, 51, 99.

18. Hagedorn, *Beyond the River*, 60–63.

19. Grant, *Personal Memoirs*, 22–27.

20. Weeks, "John P. Parker," 155–62; Sprague, *His Promised Land*, 25–70.

21. Sprague, *His Promised Land*, 90–97.

22. Weeks, "John P. Parker"; Sprague, *His Promised Land*, 127–28.

23. U.S. Census of 1880, Inhabitants of Ripley, County of Brown, State of Ohio, June 11, 1880, courtesy of UTPL.

24. Census of 1880; map of Ripley, Ohio, 1876, Brown and Co. Atlas, courtesy of UTPL; the story of Charles moving the cattle comes from Linda Settles, whose grandfather-in-law (Eugene Settles) remembers his father, Edward Settles, talking about Charles Young.

25. Census of 1880; Broadstone, *History of Greene County*, 948.

26. C. N. Young, "Biography of Col. Charles Young."

27. Census of 1880; map of Ripley, 1876.

28. Census of 1880.

29. Broadstone, *History of Greene County Ohio*, 948.

30. C. N. Young, "Biography of Col. Charles Young"; "Charles Young: The Desert and Solitary Place."

31. *Ripley Bee and Times*, December 28, 1881, 1; Stivers, *Ripley, Ohio*, 189.

32. "Ripley Union School Report," *Ripley Bee and Times*, December 28, 1881, 1; Stivers, *Ripley, Ohio*, 189.

33. *Ripley Bee and Times*, June 8, 1881, 1.

34. Stivers, *Ripley, Ohio*, 57; Glen B. Knight, "Brief History of the GAR," http://suvcw.org/gar.htm; listing of GAR commanders and encampments at http://suvcw.org/garcinc.htm.

35. Transcript of diary entry of Cora Young Wiles, February 24, 25, 26, 1881, displayed at the Ripley Museum, Ripley OH.

36. Wiles Diary, February 26, 1881.

37. Alison Gibson, UTPL, e-mail, October 10, 2002. When the schools formally integrated in 1891, many whites resisted. An economic boycott was employed against black farmers and tenants with the hope that they would leave the area, but it failed. Gerber, *Black Ohio and the Color Line*, 264.

38. *Ripley Bee and Times*, March 29, 1876, 1; Sprague, *His Promised Land*, 12.

39. A copy of this letter is in the possession of Carl Westmoreland of Ripley OH.

40. Ripley High School commencement program, June 2, 1881, courtesy of UTPL; *Ripley Bee and Times*, June 8, 1881, 1.

41. Ripley High School commencement program, June 2, 1881; *Ripley Bee and Times*, June 8, 1881.

42. Ripley High School commencement program, June 2, 1881; *Ripley Bee and Times*, June 8, 1881, 1; Weeks, "John P. Parker," 155. Several secondary sources tell the story of Young losing the valedictorian honors to a white boy because of racial bias and then later winning his West Point nomination by achieving a higher score than this same individual, named Strobridge. The first part of the story is simply wrong, since a woman in Young's class was the valedictorian, as is the second.

43. *Ripley Bee and Times*, December 28, 1881, 1, June 28, 1882, 1.

44. C. N. Young, "Biography of Col. Charles Young"; "Charles Young: The Desert and Solitary Place."

45. Charles Young's grade-book, Charles Young Papers, NAAMCC; Sprague, *His Promised Land*, 2.

46. *Ripley Bee and Times*, July 11, October 3, 1883.

47. Greene, *Early Life of Colonel Charles Young*, 9.

48. "Charles Young: The Desert and Solitary Place."

49. Purnell, "Colonel Charles Young," 5.

50. *Ripley Bee and Times*, May 2, 1883, 1.

51. Association of Graduates, *Register of Graduates and Former Cadets of the United States Military Academy*, 4-64 [hereinafter cited as *Register of Graduates (2000)*]; Official Register of the Officers and Cadets of the U.S. Military Academy (1884), 22, WPLSC [hereinafter cited as Official Register of USMA with year and pages].

52. Meier and Rudwick, *From Plantation to Ghetto*, 168-76.

53. *Ripley Bee and Times*, August 10, 1881.

54. *Ripley Bee and Times*, June 27, 1883, 1.

55. Official Register of USMA, 1884, 28; *Ripley Bee and Times*, May 7, 1884.

56. Nomination File of Charles Young, War Department Records, NARA.

57. *Ripley Bee and Times*, June 4, 1884, 1.

Beast Barracks and Plebe Year

1. West Point is the oldest continuously occupied U.S. military garrison in the country.

2. *West Point*, 1. Stoddard published this pictorial each year, with information and pictures from the four classes. It was an informal annual. Official Register of USMA, 1884, 33.

3. Obituary of Charles Young by Charles Rhodes, USMA Annual Report, June 12, 1922, WPLSC; Report of Examining Board, Lt. Col. Charles Young, July 7, 1917, Charles Young Papers, Nancy Heinl Document Collection, Washington DC.

4. *West Point*, 2.

5. Reminiscences of William Lassiter, p. 9, William Lassiter Papers, WPLSC.

6. Headquarters, USMA, West Point NY, June 24, 1884, Orders no. 156, Letter to the Adjutant General, U.S. Army, WPLSC. This letter lists all who passed the entrance exams as well as those who failed and why they failed. Some congressmen sent both a primary and an alternate candidate to West Point in case the first failed to pass the examinations.

7. Headquarters, USMA, West Point NY, June 24, 1884, Orders no. 156.

8. Official Register of USMA, 1884, 21-22.

9. *West Point*, 1.

10. Lassiter reminiscences, p. 10, Lassiter Papers.

11. Ambrose, *Duty, Honor, Country*, 222-23. Despite opposition from superintendents, hazing continued with the backing of the old graduates and surreptitious support of the faculty. It soon became associated with the spirit of West Point.

12. Lassiter reminiscences, p. 10, Lassiter Papers.

13. Ambrose, *Duty, Honor, Country,* 227–28.

14. Crackel, *Illustrated History of West Point,* 90, 166.

15. Crackel, *Illustrated History of West Point,* 90, 163.

16. Selected Documents Relating to Blacks Nominated for Appointment to the United States Military Academy During the 19th Century, 1870–1887, microfilm series M1002, NARA.

17. Crackel, *West Point,* 145.

18. Flipper, *The Colored Cadet at West Point,* xvi, 37, 164–45, 288–89.

19. Flipper, *The Colored Cadet at West Point,* 255–56.

20. Flipper, *The Colored Cadet at West Point,* 249–50.

21. Flipper, *The Colored Cadet at West Point,* 249–50.

22. Fleming, *Men and Times,* 213–31.

23. Crackel, *West Point,* 146. The first half of the next year Whitaker roomed with Charles Augustus Minnie, a black cadet from New York, but Minnie failed mathematics and was discharged in January 1878.

24. Crackel, *West Point,* 146–47.

25. 2nd Lt. Robert L. Howze, Sixth U.S. Cavalry, was awarded the Medal of Honor for bravery in action at White River, South Carolina, on January 1, 1892. *Register of Graduates (2000),* 5-30.

26. Mark Hersey memoir, pp. 2–3, Mark L. Hersey Papers, WPLSC.

27. Hersey memoir, pp. 2–3.

28. Official Register of USMA, 1884, 15; 1885, 15; 1886, 16; 1887, 16.

29. Conduct Roll of Cadets at USMA, Records of the USMA, microfilm series M1002, roll 21, NARA.

30. Merritt, "United States Military Academy," 201.

31. *Register of Graduates (2000),* 4-61 through 4-65.

32. Official Register of USMA, 1884, 30.

33. Each graduate of West Point is assigned a reference and identification number known as a Cullum number. In 1850, Bvt. Maj. Gen. George W. Cullum, class of 1833, began the ambitious work of chronicling the biographies of every graduate. He assigned number 1 to the first graduate, Joseph G. Swift, and then numbered all successive graduates in sequence. The current *Register of Graduates* and the files contained in the West Point Library Special Collections are direct descendants of Cullum's work.

34. Ledger Folio 458, Cadet Henry Jervey, class of 1888, Henry Jervey Papers, WPLSC.

35. Excerpt from June 10, 1884, letter, Rhodes, *Intimate Letters,* 1.

36. Rhodes to his parents, July 6, 1885, Charles D. Rhodes Papers, WPLSC.

37. Rhodes, *Intimate Letters,* June 22, 1885, p. 1.

38. Rhodes to his parents, July 2, 1885, Rhodes Papers.

39. Register of Delinquencies, USMA, Book 23, 1884–1888, p. 368, WPLSC.

40. Register of Delinquencies, USMA, Book 23, 1884–1888, p. 368.

41. Rhodes to his parents, June 17, 1885, Rhodes Papers.

42. Official Register of USMA, 1884, 30.

43. Academic Rankings of Cadets at West Point, January 1885, microfilm series M1002, roll 21, NARA. Only those who passed the exam were ranked. Therefore, ninety-one passed English and seventy-five passed the more difficult mathematics test. Those who flunked either test in the first semester of plebe year were separated from West Point.

44. Official Register of USMA, 1884, 22.

45. In addition to the sixty-nine cadets admitted in June 1884, there were two foreign cadets and another ten who had reported in September 1884 or were turned back from the previous year.

46. Report of Deficient Cadets, Headquarters, USMA, West Point NY, June 10, 1885, WPLSC.

47. Report of Deficient Cadets, June 10, 1885. Of seventeen plebes of the class of 1888 found deficient in academics, six were recommended to be "turned back to join the next class." All six were found deficient in math, and two were foreign students. Five of these six graduated with Young in the bottom ten of the class of 1889.

48. "Charles Young: The Desert and Solitary Place."

Plebe Year Again

1. Rhodes later said the collection of several hundred letters was "written at odd moments, without thought of future preservation, and couched in that happy-go-lucky literary style, which one might expect between mother and son" (*Intimate Letters*, foreword). His mother saved every letter and returned them to Rhodes twenty-five years after he graduated. Rhodes, who retired as a major general in 1929, edited and published the letters in *Intimate Letters of a West Point Cadet* for the class of 1889 on the fiftieth anniversary of their entrance into West Point, in 1935. The letters were later donated to the West Point Library's Special Collections. Rhodes edited the letters heavily for publication in his book. Wherever possible, I have used the original letters, a few of which are missing from the collection.

2. Rhodes to his parents, June 17, 1885, Rhodes Papers.

3. Official Register of USMA, 1886, 17–19, 28.

4. W. A. Hare to J. P. Green, June 28, 1885, John P. Green Papers, WRHS. Green served as an Ohio state representative and senator in the late

nineteenth century. I first read the text of this letter in Carhart, "African-American West Pointers in the Nineteenth Century," 226.

5. Rhodes to his parents, July 5, 1885, Rhodes Papers.

6. Reminiscences of Edward F. McGlachlin Jr., p. 20, Edward F. McGlachlin Jr. Papers, WPLSC.

7. Register of Delinquencies, USMA, Book 23, 1884–1888, p. 368, WPLSC.

8. McGlachlin reminiscences, p. 22, McGlachlin Papers.

9. McGlachlin reminiscences, p. 19, McGlachlin Papers.

10. Post Order 129, July 23, 1885, Post Order 138, August 5, 1885, Post Order 140, August 7, 1885, Post Orders Book 11, WPLSC.

11. McGlachlin reminiscences, p. 22, McGlachlin Papers.

12. Lassiter reminiscences, p. 11, Lassiter Papers.

13. Register of Delinquencies, USMA, Book 23, 1884–1888, p. 368, WPLSC.

14. Rhodes to his parents, July 5, 1885, Rhodes Papers.

15. Lassiter reminiscences, p. 11, Lassiter Papers. Young and Pershing served remarkably similar duty assignments after graduation, including tours on the western frontier with Buffalo Soldier regiments that earned Pershing the nickname "Black Jack." They also shared similar duty as professors of military science at universities, as military attachés overseas, fighting guerrillas in the Philippines, and chasing Pancho Villa in Mexico. While Young retired on the eve of World War I as a colonel, Pershing went on to command the American Expeditionary Force in Europe and earned four stars.

16. Rhodes to his parents, August 29, 1885, Rhodes Papers.

17. Rhodes to his parents, August 29, 1885.

18. Battalion Organization, January 1886, Charles Rhodes USMA Scrapbook, vol. 2, Rhodes Papers.

19. Battalion Organization, January 1886, Rhodes Scrapbook, Rhodes Papers.

20. Heitman, *Historical Register*, 2:193.

21. Col. Malvern-Hill Barnum to Col. Allen J. Greer, April 19, 1919, AWC-127-21, Army War College, Carlisle PA. Although Barnum joined the Third Cavalry after graduation, he transferred to the Buffalo Soldiers Tenth Cavalry in 1894. He was wounded charging San Juan Hill with the Tenth in Cuba during the Spanish-American War.

22. Battalion Organization, January 1886, Rhodes Scrapbook, Rhodes Papers.

23. Academic Rankings of Cadets at West Point, January 1886, microfilm series M1002, roll 21, NARA.

24. Academic Rankings of Cadets at West Point, January 1886, microfilm series M1002, roll 21, NARA.

25. Rhodes to his parents, January 10, 1886, Rhodes Papers.

26. Rhodes to his parents, January 25, 1886, Rhodes Papers.

27. Rhodes to his parents, February 7, 1886, Rhodes Papers.

28. Godson, "History of West Point," 47.

29. Rhodes to his parents, February 21, 1886, Rhodes Papers.

30. Godson, "History of West Point," 47; Todd, *Cadet Gray*, 93.

31. McGlachlin reminiscences, p. 25, McGlachlin Papers.

32. Rhodes to his parents, April 18, 1886, Rhodes Papers; *Register of Graduates (2000)*, p. 4-24.

33. Todd, *Cadet Gray*, 93.

34. McGlachlin reminiscences, p. 26, McGlachlin Papers.

35. McGlachlin reminiscences, p. 25, McGlachlin Papers.

36. McGlachlin reminiscences, p. 25, McGlachlin Papers.

37. McGlachlin reminiscences, p. 27, McGlachlin Papers.

38. Rhodes to his parents, June 1, 1886, Rhodes Papers.

39. Official Register of USMA, 1886, 17–18; McGlachlin reminiscences, p. 23, McGlachlin Papers.

40. Leon, *Twain and West Point*, 19–79.

41. Leon, *Twain and West Point*, 66.

42. Leon, *Twain and West Point*, 67.

43. Leon, *Twain and West Point*, 71.

44. McGlachlin reminiscences, p. 22, McGlachlin Papers.

45. Rhodes to his parents, June 12, 1886, Rhodes Papers.

46. Post Order 94, June 14, 1886, Post Orders Book 11, p. 220, WPLSC. Young's other classmates were granted leave on separate post orders.

47. *Ripley Bee*, June 30, 1886.

48. Conduct Roll of Cadets, NARA. There were some months that he earned demerits and then received credits to cancel them out, bringing his monthly total to zero.

Yearling Upperclassman

1. Headquarters, USMA, West Point NY, June 12, 1886, Orders no. 92, author's collection.

2. Rhodes to his parents, July 7, 1886, Rhodes Papers.

3. Rhodes to his parents, March 5, 1887, Rhodes Papers.

4. Headquarters, USMA, West Point NY, August 31, 1886, Orders no. 147, author's collection.

5. McGlachlin reminiscences, p. 26, McGlachlin Papers.

6. After graduation, Webster was awarded the Treasury Department's Silver Lifesaving Medal in 1890 for rescuing a lighthouse keeper and his wife from drowning in New York Harbor. USMA Annual Report, January 9, 1932, pp. 165–68, WPLSC.

7. Rhodes to his parents, August 28, 1886.

8. Headquarters, USMA, West Point NY, September 16, 1886, Orders no. 159, author's collection.

9. Rhodes to his parents, August 29, 1886, Rhodes Papers.

10. Rhodes, *Intimate Letters*, September 19, 1896, p. 5, and April 24, 1887, p. 6.

11. Headquarters, USMA, West Point NY, September 2, 1886, Orders no. 148, author's collection; Rhodes, *Intimate Letters*, October 17, 1886, p. 6.

12. *Register of Graduates (2000)*, p. 4-39.

13. Academic Rankings of the 3rd Class, West Point, June 13, 1887, microfilm series M1002, roll 21, NARA.

14. McGlachlin reminiscences, p. 30, McGlachlin Papers.

15. Rhodes to his parents, January 15, 1887, Rhodes Papers.

16. *Register of Graduates (2000)*, p. 4-66.

17. Headquarters, USMA, West Point NY, December 28, 1886, Orders no. 215, author's collection.

18. Rhodes to his parents, October 31, 1886, Rhodes Papers.

19. Rhodes to his parents, November 21, 1886, Rhodes Papers.

20. Rhodes to his parents, November 13, 1886, Rhodes Papers.

21. King, "Cadet Life at West Point," 215.

22. McGlachlin reminiscences, p. 25, McGlachlin Papers.

23. King, "Cadet Life at West Point," 216; Rhodes, *Intimate Letters*, March 3, 1889, p. 21.

24. King, "Cadet Life at West Point," 217.

25. Rhodes to his parents, May 15, 1887, Rhodes Papers.

26. Rhodes to his parents, May 15, 1887.

27. C. N. Young, "Biography of Col. Charles Young."

28. Leon, *Twain and West Point*, 71.

29. Crackel, *West Point*, 157.

30. Leon, *Twain and West Point*, 73; Rhodes, *Intimate Letters*, May 1, 1887, p. 8.

31. Leon, *Twain and West Point*, 73–75.

32. Leon, *Twain and West Point*, 75.

33. Leon, *Twain and West Point*, 75.

34. Rhodes to his parents, December 7, 1885, Rhodes Papers.

35. Rhodes to his parents, October 3, 1886, Rhodes Papers.

36. Merritt, "United States Military Academy," 201.

37. Flipper, *The Colored Cadet at West Point*, 107.

38. John H. Alexander to J. P. Green, February 8, 1885, Green Papers; Gatewood, "John Hanks Alexander," 121.

39. Academic Rankings of the 3rd Class, West Point, June 13, 1887, microfilm series M1002, roll 21, NARA; Conduct Roll of Cadets, NARA.

40. Official Register of USMA, 1887, 15.

41. *Register of Graduates (2000)*, p. 4-63.

42. Rhodes to his parents, June 3, 1888, Rhodes Papers.

43. Rhodes to his parents, April 3, 1887, Rhodes Papers.

44. Rhodes to his parents, May 1, 1887, Rhodes Papers.

45. Post Order 105, June 24, 1887, Post Orders Book 11, WPLSC; *Register of Graduates (2000)*, p. 4-63.

46. *Register of Graduates (2000)*, p. 4-63.

47. Alexander died unexpectedly in 1893, shortly after completing his first duty assignment with the Ninth Cavalry. He had just been assigned as a professor of military science and tactics at Wilberforce University in Ohio when he suffered a massive heart attack and died. His death would shift the mantle to Young as the Regular Army's lone surviving African American graduate of West Point. Gatewood, "John Hanks Alexander," 123.

48. Godson, "History of West Point," 48.

Cow Year Alone

1. Ambrose, *Duty, Honor, Country*, 220-21.

2. Headquarters, USMA, West Point NY, June 12, 1966, Orders no. 92, author's collection.

3. Bulletin no. 82, Minutes of the 50th Anniversary Reunion held at West Point June 9, 1939, Alexander R. Piper Papers, WPLSC.

4. Alexander Piper to Ada Young, July 13, 1939, Young Papers, Coleman Collection.

5. Obituary of Alexander Ross Piper, *Assembly Magazine*, January 1953, 47.

6. Piper obituary, 47.

7. Alexander Piper to Ada Young, July 13, 1939.

8. McGlachlin reminiscences, p. 31, McGlachlin Papers.

9. McGlachlin reminiscences, p. 31, McGlachlin Papers.

10. Rhodes to his parents, August 28, 1887, Rhodes Papers.

11. *Register of Graduates (2000)*, p. 4-30; Crackel, *West Point*, 157.

12. Headquarters, USMA, West Point NY, September 4, 1886, Orders no. 150, author's collection.

13. Crackel, *West Point*, 149.

14. Obituary of Charles Young by Charles D. Rhodes, USMA Annual Report, June 12, 1922, WPLSC.

15. Dance Card, Rhodes Scrapbook, vol. 2, Rhodes Papers.

16. Rhodes, *Intimate Letters*, February 24, 1889, p. 20.

17. Official Register of USMA, 1887, 31.

18. Obituary of Delamere Skerrett by Charles D. Rhodes, USMA Annual Report, June 10, 1939, WPLSC.

19. *Army and Navy Journal*, October 8, 1887, WPLSC.

20. *Army and Navy Journal*, December 3, 1887, WPLSC.

21. Rhodes to his parents, November 6, December 11 and 24, 1887, Rhodes Papers.

22. McGlachlin reminiscences, p. 31, McGlachlin Papers.

23. Conduct Roll of Cadets, NARA.

24. Academic Rankings of the 2nd Class, West Point, January 11, 1888, roll 21, M1002, NARA; Conduct Roll of Cadets, NARA.

25. Rhodes to his parents, January 6 and 8, 1888, Rhodes Papers.

26. Rhodes to his parents, January 15, 1888, Rhodes Papers.

27. Sladen served with the Tactical Department from 1900 to 1904, as the commandant of cadets from 1911 to 1914, and as superintendent from 1922 to 1926. He retired a major general in 1931. *Register of Graduates (2000)*, p. 4-66.

28. *Register of Graduates (2000)*, p. 4-40; McGlachlin reminiscences, p. 29, McGlachlin Papers.

29. Rhodes, *Intimate Letters*, February 5, 1888, p. 12; *Register of Graduates (2000)*, p. 5-18.

30. Rhodes to his parents, February 12, 1888, Rhodes Papers.

31. Rhodes to his parents, February 18, 1888, Rhodes Papers.

32. McGlachlin reminiscences, p. 33, McGlachlin Papers.

33. Rhodes, *Intimate Letters*, September 4, 1887, p. 9.

34. Rhodes to his parents, November 6, 1887, Rhodes Papers.

35. Rhodes to his parents, September 18, 1887, Rhodes Papers.

36. Rhodes to his parents, December 4, 1887, Rhodes Papers.

37. Rhodes to his parents, September 18, 1887, May 20, 1888, Rhodes Papers.

38. Rhodes to his parents, October 31, 1887, Rhodes Papers.

39. Rhodes Scrapbook, vol. 1, Written Request by Edwin T. Cole, May 2, 1888, Rhodes Papers.

40. Ambrose, *Duty, Honor, Country*, 221.

41. McGlachlin reminiscences, p. 34, McGlachlin Papers.

42. See www.theirvingsociety.org.uk.

43. McGlachlin reminiscences, p. 34, McGlachlin Papers.

44. Rhodes to his parents, March 25, 1888, Rhodes Papers.

45. Rhodes to his parents, March 25, 1888.

46. McGlachlin reminiscences, p. 31, McGlachlin Papers.

47. Academic Rankings of the 2nd Class, West Point, June 13, 1888, microfilm series M1002, roll 21, NARA.

48. McGlachlin reminiscences, p. 33, McGlachlin Papers.

49. Purnell, "Colonel Charles Young," 6.

50. James Abbot McNeill Whistler entered West Point in 1851 with the class of 1855 but was kicked out after his third year for failing chemistry and for excessive demerits. His father was a graduate of West Point, and his mother was a sister to an academy graduate. *Register of Graduates (2000)*, p. 4-36.

51. Register of Delinquencies, USMA, Book 23, 1884–1888, p. 487, WPLSC.

52. The National Afro-American Museum and Cultural Center in Wilberforce, Ohio, discovered this valuable portfolio in a closet of the Charles Young house in Zenia, Ohio, and it was conserved through the support of West Point and the Association of Graduates. The maps can still be found on file in the National Archives, and another of Liberia from a later attaché tour resides at the Young Papers at NAAMCC.

53. Charles Young Papers at NAAMCC; handwriting analysis by John Birznieks, May 2004.

54. Rhodes, *Intimate Letters*, April 7, 1888, February 10, 1889, pp. 14, 20.

55. Rhodes to his parents, June 13, 1888, Rhodes Papers.

56. Rhodes to his parents, June 24, July 1, 1888, Rhodes Papers.

57. Rhodes to his parents, June 13, 1888.

Firstie Year and Graduation

1. Todd, *Cadet Gray*, 38–39.

2. Two such albums purchased by class members reside in the Class Album Collection, WPLSC.

3. USMA Class of 'Eighty Nine Photograph List, Pach Brothers, 841 Broadway, New York, Rhodes Scrapbook, vol. 1, Rhodes Papers.

4. Official Register of USMA, 1889, 29.

5. Official Register of USMA, 1889, 29.

6. Rhodes to his parents, September 22, 1888, Rhodes Papers.

7. Rhodes, *Intimate Letters*, October 7, 1888, p. 18.

8. Rhodes to his parents, September 30, 1888, Rhodes Papers.

9. It took Johnson and his cohorts one night, working in fifteen-

minute intervals between sentry passes, to complete this engineering feat; it took the post engineer four days to get it back down. Pappas, "General MacArthur and the Reveille Cannon."

10. Rhodes to his parents, November 10, 1888, Rhodes Papers.

11. Rhodes to his parents, December 9, 1888, Rhodes Papers.

12. At graduation, Langhorne, like Young, joined the cavalry. They later shared similar assignments in the army, including postings in the Philippines and duty as military attachés. *Register of Graduates (2000)*, p. 4-65; Mary Waller Langhorne, obituary of George Tayloe Langhorne, *Assembly Magazine*, summer 1962, 88.

13. Academic Rankings of Cadets at West Point, microfilm series M1002, roll 21, NARA.

14. Rhodes, *Intimate Letters*, January 13, 1889, p. 19; USMA Staff Records, Book 13, May 3, 1889, pp. 249–50, WPLSC.

15. Rhodes, *Intimate Letters*, May 9, 1886, p. 3.

16. Rhodes to his parents, January 27, 1889, Rhodes Papers.

17. Heitman, *Historical Register*, 1:865, 1068, 2:614–15.

18. McGlachlin reminiscences, p. 34, McGlachlin Papers.

19. Rhodes, *Intimate Letters*, March 30, 1889, p. 21.

20. Rhodes to his parents, November 10, 1888, Rhodes Papers.

21. Rhodes to his parents, February 10, 1889, Rhodes Papers.

22. Rhodes, *Intimate Letters*, February 24, 1889, p. 20.

23. Rhodes to his parents, March 10, 1889, Rhodes Papers.

24. Rhodes to his parents, April 28, 1888, Rhodes Papers.

25. Rhodes to his parents, May 4, 1888, Rhodes Papers.

26. Rhodes to his parents, January 27, 1889, Rhodes Papers.

27. *Cleveland Gazette*, February 16, 1889, 2.

28. Rhodes to his parents, January 27, 1889, Rhodes Papers.

29. E. H. Lawson, "One Out of the Twelve Million," *Washington Post*, May 26, 1829, 11.

30. Lawson, "One Out of the Twelve Million," p. 11.

31. Obituary of Delamere Skerrett by Charles D. Rhodes, USMA Annual Report, June 10, 1939, WPLSC.

32. Register of Delinquencies, USMA, Book 24, 1889–1893, p. 218, WPLSC.

33. Register of Delinquencies, USMA, Book 24, p. 218.

34. Obituary of Charles Young by Charles D. Rhodes, USMA Annual Report, June 12, 1922, WPLSC.

35. Obituary of Charles Young by Charles D. Rhodes.

36. Rhodes to his parents, June 9, 1889, Rhodes Papers.

37. Rhodes, *Intimate Letters*, 25. Fifteen years later, as the superintendent

of Grant and Sequoia National Parks, Young built a fence to protect the General Sherman Tree from trampling by tourists.

38. Rhodes, *Intimate Letters*, 25.

39. Memoir of William W. Harts, p. 9, William Wright Harts Papers, WPLSC.

40. Before the newly commissioned officers of the class of 1889 scattered across the country, they took a ferry to New York City for one last class dinner at the Hoffman House and a Broadway theater performance. According to Rhodes, the favorites on the faculty were on hand to help them celebrate, including "Pete" (Peter S. Michie), the "Com" (commandant, Lt. Col. Hamilton S. Hawkins), (Edgar W.) "Poppy" Bass, "Prof" (James) Mercur, (Samuel E.) "Sammy" Tillman, (Joseph) "Joe" Dorst, "Spurge" (William F. Spurgin), "the Goat" (?), (Daniel L.) "Danny" Tate, and "Sir" John Totten. Their presence no longer brought "terrors to '89; on this night of nights, dignity was in the discard!" Rhodes, *Intimate Letters*, 25.

41. USMA Staff Records, Book 13, June 8, 1889, pp. 252–56, WPLSC.

42. USMA Staff Records, Book 13, June 10, 1889, pp. 257–60, WPLSC.

43. Goethals quoted in Romero, *I Too Am America*, 190.

44. Dupuy, *Harper Encyclopedia of Military Biography*, 283. Three of Young's classmates assisted Goethals in building the Panama Canal. Eben Winslow, who graduated first in his class, designed all of the major fortifications for the Panama Canal. Chester Harding served as the chief engineer for the construction of the Gatun Locks and succeeded Goethals as the governor of the Canal Zone. Like Goethals, both Winslow and Harding taught civil engineering at West Point as lieutenants before shipping out to Panama. Ben Johnson resigned his commission shortly after graduation, became a civil engineer, and served under Harding as the construction superintendent of the Gatun Locks. *Register of Graduates (2000)*, p. 4-65; Fishburne, "USMA Class Celebrates Centennial Reunion," 5.

45. USMA Staff Records, Book 13, August 31, 1889, p. 297, WPLSC.

46. An officer was commissioned as an additional second lieutenant in the regiment to which he was assigned until a formal vacancy opened, at which time he became a second lieutenant.

47. Lt. Charles Young to the Adjutant General, September 14, 1889, Selected ACP Branch Records, Charles Young, Record Group 94, NARA.

48. Young to Adjutant General, October 6, 1889, and Adjutant General to Young, October 16, 1889, Selected ACP Branch Records, NARA.

49. Memorandum, Adjutant General, Washington, October 29, 1889, Selected ACP Branch Records, NARA; Special Order no. 254, Headquarters

of the Army, Adjutant General's Office, Washington, October 31, 1889, Selected ACP Branch Records, NARA.

50. The regimental commander, Col. Joseph G. Tilford, was on leave, and the regimental lieutenant colonel, George B. Sanford, was at Fort Leavenworth.

51. Maj. G. V. Henry to the Adjutant General, January 30, 1890, Selected ACP Branch Records, NARA.

52. *Register of Graduates (2000)*, p. 4-40.

53. Memorandum, Adjutant General, Washington, January 30, 1890, Selected ACP Branch Records, NARA.

Epilogue

1. Charles Young to Delamere Skerrett, July 23, 1915, Young Papers, WPLSC.

2. The numbers are less impressive if we add the numbers of the class of 1889 who did not graduate: forty-eight. Young listed as friends only two from this group.

3. Maj. Charles Young to Capt. Alexander Piper, July 26, 1915, in Romero, *I Too Am America*, 190.

4. Brig. Gen. John J. Pershing, Headquarter Punitive Expedition, to Adjutant General of the Army, August 21, 1916, Young Papers, Coleman Collection.

5. Col. Charles Young to Charles I. Smith Jr., January 15, 1919, Young Papers, NAAMCC.

6. Charles Young to Alexander Piper, February 17, 1919, Young Papers, WPLSC.

7. Col. Charles Young to Sen. Atlee Pomerene, August 20, 1918, Young Papers, Coleman Collection. Pomerene was the chairman of the Senate Committee on Privileges and Elections, and Young was writing to him to defend his reputation against rumors that he was pro-German.

Bibliography

Primary Sources

Coleman Collection, Akron OH
Charles Young Papers.

Nancy Heinl Document Collection, Washington DC
Charles Young Papers.

National Afro-American Museum and Cultural Center, Wilberforce OH
Charles Young Papers.

National Archives and Records Administration, College Park MD
Academic Rankings of Cadets at West Point, 1884–89. Microfilm series M1002, roll 21.

Conduct Roll of Cadets at USMA, Records of the United States Military Academy. Microfilm series M1002, roll 21.

Selected Appointment, Commission, and Personal Branch Records. Record Group 94.

Selected Documents Relating to Blacks Nominated for Appointment to the United States Military Academy During the 19th Century, 1870–1887. Microfilm series M1002.

Summary of Units and Miscellaneous Service Cards, 5th U.S. Colored Heavy Artillery. Microfilm series M1818, roll 108.

War Department Records. Record Group 107.

Union Township Public Library, Ripley OH
Map of Ripley, Ohio, 1876.

U.S. Census of 1870.

U.S. Census of 1880.

Western Reserve Historical Society, Cleveland OH
J. P. Green Papers.

West Point Library Special Collections, West Point NY

John H. Alexander Papers.

Harry H. Bandholtz Papers.

Malvern-Hill Barnum Papers.

Walter A. Bethel Papers.

Clement A. F. Flagler Papers.

William S. Graves Papers.

William G. Haan Papers.

Ralph Harrison Papers.

William Wright Harts Papers.

Mark L. Hersey Papers.

Henry Jervey Papers.

George T. Langhorne Papers.

William Lassiter Papers.

Joseph D. Leitch Papers.

Edward F. McGlachlin Jr. Papers.

James E. Normoyle Papers.

Official Register of the Officers and Cadets of the U.S. Military Academy. West Point NY. Vol. 7, 1878–1887. Vol. 8, 1884–1887.

Alexander R. Piper Papers.

Post Orders Book 11, USMA, 1885.

Register of Delinquencies, USMA. Book 23, 1884–1888. Book 24, 1889–1893.

Report of Deficient Cadets. Headquarters, USMA, West Point NY, June 10, 1885.

Charles D. Rhodes Papers.

Delamere Skerrett Papers.

John R. M. Taylor Papers.

USMA Annual Reports.

USMA Staff Records, Book 13.

Frank D. Webster Papers.

West Point Class of 1888 Papers.

Charles Young Papers.

Secondary Sources

Ambrose, Stephen E. *Duty, Honor, Country: A History of West Point*. Baltimore: Johns Hopkins University Press, 1966.

Association of Graduates. *Register of Graduates and Former Cadets of the United States Military Academy*. West Point NY: Association of Graduates, 2000.

Berlin, Ira, ed. *Freedom: A Documentary History of Emancipation, 1861–1867. Series II, The Black Military Experience*. New York: Cambridge University Press, 1980.

Berlin, Ira, Barbara J. Fields, Steven F. Miller, Joseph P. Reidy, and Leslie S. Rowland. *Slaves No More*. New York: Cambridge University Press, 1992.

Broadstone, M. A., ed. *History of Greene County, Ohio*. Vol. 2. Indianapolis: B. F. Bowen, 1918.

Calvert, Jean, and John Klee. *The Towns of Mason County—Their Past in Pictures*. Maysville KY: Maysville and Mason County Library Historical and Scientific Society, 1986.

Carhart, Tom. "African-American West Pointers in the Nineteenth Century." Ph.D. diss., Princeton University, 1998.

Crackel, Theodore J. *Illustrated History of West Point*. New York: Harry N. Abrams, 1991.

———. *West Point: A Bicentennial History*. Lawrence: University Press of Kansas, 2002.

Dillard, Walter Scott. "The United States Military Academy, 1865–1900: The Uncertain Years." Ph.D. diss., University of Washington, 1972.

Dupuy, Trevor N. *The Harper Encyclopedia of Military Biography*. New York: Castle Books, 1992.

Dyer, Frederick H. *A Compendium of the War of the Rebellion*. Des Moines IA: Dyer, 1908.

Fields, Barbara J. *Slavery and Freedom in the Middle Ground*. New Haven: Yale University Press, 1985.

Fishburne, E. G., Lt. Col. "USMA Class Celebrates Centennial Reunion." *Pointer View*, April 14, 1989, 5.

Fleming, Thomas J. *The Men and Times of the United States Military Academy*. New York: William Morrow, 1969.

Flipper, Henry Ossian. *The Colored Cadet at West Point*. Lincoln: University of Nebraska Press, 1998.

Fox-Genovese, Elizabeth. *Within the Plantation Household: Black and White Women of the Old South*. Chapel Hill: University of North Carolina Press, 1988.

Frederic, Francis. *Slave Life in Virginia and Kentucky; or, Fifty Years of Slavery in the Southern States of America*. London: Wertheim, Macintosh, and Hunt, 1863.

Gatewood, Willard B., Jr. "John Hanks Alexander of Arkansas, Second Black Graduate of West Point." *Arkansas Historical Quarterly* 41 (summer 1982): 103–28.

Gerber, David A. *Black Ohio and the Color Line*. Chicago: University of Illinois Press, 1976.

Gladstone, William A. *Men of Color*. Gettysburg PA: Thomas Publications, 1993.

Godson, William F. H., Jr. "The History of West Point, 1852–1902." Ph.D. diss., Temple University, 1934.

Grant, Ulysses S. *The Personal Memoirs of Ulysses S. Grant*. Old Saybrook CT: Konecky & Konecky, 1992.

Greene, Robert E. *Colonel Charles Young: Soldier and Diplomat*. Washington DC: Robert E. Greene, 1985.

———. *Early Life of Colonel Charles Young: 1864–1889*. Washington DC: Howard University, Department of History Student Publication Series, 1973.

Hagedorn, Ann. *Beyond the River: The Untold Story of the Heroes of the Underground Railroad*. New York: Simon and Schuster, 2003.

Harrison, Lowell H., *The Civil War in Kentucky*. Lexington: University Press of Kentucky, 1975.

Heitman, Francis B. *Historical Register and Dictionary of the U.S. Army*. 2 vols. Washington DC: Government Printing Office, 1903.

King, Charles B. "Cadet Life at West Point." *Harper's New Monthly Magazine*, July 1887, 197–219.

Klotter, James C. *Our Kentucky: A Study of the Bluegrass State*. Lexington: University Press of Kentucky, 1992.

Leon, Philip W. *Mark Twain and West Point*. Toronto: ECW Press, 1996.

Meier, August, and Elliott Rudwick, *From Plantation to Ghetto*. New York: Hill and Wang, 1970.

Merritt, Wesley. "The United States Military Academy at West Point." *The Youth's Companion*, May 5, 1887, 201.

Miller, Caroline R. *Slavery in Mason County, Kentucky: A Century of Records, 1788–1888*. Vols. 1 and 2. Maysville KY: National Underground Railroad Museum, 1988.

Pappas, George S. "General MacArthur and the Reveille Cannon." *Assembly*, July/August 2001, 60–66.

Purnell, John H. "Colonel Charles Young, U.S.A., Soldier, Diplomat, Philanthropist, Man of Culture." *The Oracle* 64 (winter 1979): 5–8.

Rhodes, Charles Dudley. *Intimate Letters of a West Point Cadet*. Self-published, 1935.

Romero, Patricia W., ed. *I Too Am America: Documents from 1619 to the Present*. New York: Publishers Company, 1968.

Shaffer, Donald R. "In the Shadow of the Old Constitution: Black Civil

War Veterans and the Persistence of Slave Marriage Customs." In *Southern Families at War: Loyalty and Conflict in the Civil War South*, edited by Catherine Clinton, 59–75. New York: Oxford University Press, 2000.

Sprague, Stuart Seely, ed. *His Promised Land: The Autobiography of John P. Parker*. New York: Norton, 1996.

Stivers, Elise Bamback. *Ripley, Ohio: Its History and Families*. Ripley OH: Self-published, 1965.

Stuckey, Sterling "Through the Prism of Folklore: The Black Ethos of Slavery." In *American Negro Slavery*, edited by Allen Weinstein and Frank Otto Gatell, 134–47. New York: Oxford University Press, 1973.

Todd, Frederick P. *Cadet Gray*. New York: Sterling, 1855.

Weeks, Louis. "John P. Parker: Black Abolitionist Entrepreneur, 1827–1900." *Ohio History* 80 (1988): 155–62.

West Point. New York: Hart and Stoddard, 1888.

Wright, George. "Afro-Americans." *Kentucky Encyclopedia*. Lexington: University Press of Kentucky, 1992.

Index